JOB SAVVY

HOW TO BE A SUCCESS AT WORK

LaVerne Ludden, Ed.D.

How to Be a Success at Work

© 1998 by JIST Works

Published by JIST Works, Inc.
720 N. Park Avenue
Indianapolis, IN 46202-3490
Phone: 317-264-3720 Fax: 317-264-3709 E-mail: jistworks@aol.com
World Wide Web Address: http://www.jist.com

Other books by LaVerne Ludden

Franchise Opportunities Handbook
Back to School: A College Guide for Adults
Luddens' Adult Guide to Colleges and Universities (with Marsha Ludden)
Mind Your Own Business (with Bonnie Maitlen)

See the back of this book for additional JIST titles and ordering information.
Quantity discounts are available.

Cover Design by Honeymoon Image & Design
Illustrations by Chris Ludden

Printed in the United States of America

1 2 3 4 5 6 7 8 9   02 01 00 99 98 97

ISBN 1-56370-304-1

JOB SAVVY

HOW TO BE A SUCCESS AT WORK

LaVerne Ludden, Ed.D.

How to Be a Success at Work

© 1998 by JIST Works

Published by JIST Works, Inc.
720 N. Park Avenue
Indianapolis, IN 46202-3490
Phone: 317-264-3720 Fax: 317-264-3709 E-mail: jistworks@aol.com
World Wide Web Address: http://www.jist.com

Other books by LaVerne Ludden

Franchise Opportunities Handbook
Back to School: A College Guide for Adults
Luddens' Adult Guide to Colleges and Universities (with Marsha Ludden)
Mind Your Own Business (with Bonnie Maitlen)

See the back of this book for additional JIST titles and ordering information.
Quantity discounts are available.

Cover Design by Honeymoon Image & Design
Illustrations by Chris Ludden

Printed in the United States of America

1 2 3 4 5 6 7 8 9   02 01 00 99 98 97

We have been careful to provide accurate information throughout this book, but it is possible that errors and omissions have been introduced. Please consider this in making any career plans or other important decisions. Trust your own judgment above all else and in all things.

ISBN 1-56370-304-1

About This Book

This is a book about keeping a job and getting ahead. Based on research into what employers actually look for in the people who succeed or fail, *Job Savvy* is designed to develop critical job survival skills, increase productivity, and improve job satisfaction and success. Using a workbook approach, many in-the-book activities are provided to reinforce key points and develop new job survival skills and plans. The narrative is easy to read and informative and uses good graphic design, many examples, checklists, case studies, and section summaries.

This is the second edition of this book. Two chapters have been added: one on trends in the workforce, and another on customer relations. In addition, more recent research about job skills have been included. There have been changes in the workplace since the first edition and these changes are presented and their implications reviewed. Everything that made the first book popular remains, so you get the best of the original along with many improvements.

Why People Need to Improve Their Basic Job Skills

The years ahead are projected to be a time of labor market opportunity and challenge for most workers. Some of these trends include:

■ People will work in more varied ways as permanent employees, temporary employees, and independent contractors.

■ Increasing competition among businesses will require changes in operations, thus requiring more flexibility in workers.

■ Many new and existing jobs will require higher levels of technical skills.

■ The amount of education and training required for jobs will increase.

■ Employers will expect their employees to be more productive and obtain better results in more complex jobs.

■ More job and career changes are anticipated for the average worker.

All of these changes will require a person who is better prepared than most workers have been in the past. The biggest need, according to most employers and labor market experts, is for workers to have good "basic" skills. These include having basic academic skills and the ability to communicate, adapt to new situations, and solve problems. While these and other related skills are not technical skills in the traditional sense, they have everything to do with long-term success on the job. And this is what this book is about.

A Different Point of View

You will find numerous references in *Job Savvy* to the studies and research of psychologists, sociologists, and other labor market professionals, yet this is *not* an academic book. Instead, this information has been used to form the basis for a practical and useful handbook for a working person—or one who soon plans to enter the world of work. Many employers have asked for such a book to give them a tool to encourage their new workers to succeed on the job. And because the author has been both an employer and a trainer of new employees, he brings a unique and helpful point of view that will bridge the gap between an employer's and an employee's expectations. The result of this is increased job savvy where, we believe, both will win.

A Parable

An explorer was once asked what he most disliked about the wilderness. "Is it the wolves?" "No," he replied, "It's the mosquitoes." In a similar way, many people fail on the job as a result of the little problems, not the big ones. This book will help you identify and avoid both, so you can be the best employee you can be.

Table of Contents

Chapter 1

Work Today . . . and Tomorrow

Did you know that most of us spend almost 95,000 hours of our lives working? Work is how we earn the money to pay for our material needs, such as food, housing, travel, and entertainment. Work satisfies many of our psychological needs, such as the need for self-fulfillment and self-esteem. And work fulfills our needs for human interaction and friendship. Because work is such a major part of our lives, it's important to have a basic understanding about work in today's society. In this chapter, we'll look at the labor force, occupations, the workplace, and the structure of work.

Your Work Experience

In the space below, briefly describe your last three jobs. Were you employed full-time or part-time? Were you hired by the company you worked for, or were you assigned by a temporary agency? How large was the company in terms of numbers of employees and customers, amount of sales, and locations? What types of technology did you use on the job?

1. _____
   _____
   _____
   _____

2. _____
   _____
   _____
   _____

3. _____
   _____
   _____
   _____

The Labor Force, 2005

The labor force refers to those people who are available and want to work. Anyone who is looking for a job or working at a job is a member of the labor force. You'll be a more effective worker if you understand some of the changes that are occurring in the labor force.[1]

1. **The labor force is growing more slowly than before.** The labor force grew 16 percent annually from 1982 to 1993. But it is expected to grow only 12 percent annually through the year 2005. This slower rate of growth will create more demand for workers in business. It will be particularly difficult for many businesses to find workers for minimum wage jobs. This may spur higher participation of younger workers (16 to 19 years old) in the workforce. Today, about 52 percent of this age group

is in the labor force. Many businesses now recruit 14- and 15-year-olds because they are willing to work for the minimum wage. It's likely that there won't be much competition for jobs that require little education and offer lower wages.

2. **More women are entering the workforce.** Women now account for 46 percent of workers in the labor force, and this is expected to increase to 48 percent by 2005. This is a dramatic change from 1969, when only 38 percent of the workforce was female.[2] Women's participation in the workforce has had a great impact on businesses. They have become more concerned about childcare, family leave, flex-time, job sharing, sexual harassment, and other issues. The changing view of women in the workplace also has changed how many organizations view the role of men within the family. This has created a demand among female and male workers for "family friendly" employment practices. Many positive changes in the workplace have resulted from the increased participation of women, and this trend is likely to continue.

3. **The labor force is aging.** The Baby Boom generation makes up a large portion of the labor force. By 2005, this group will be 45 to 64 years old. Workers in this age group typically are the most productive. It's likely that the graying of the workforce will force businesses to rethink old retirement policies and to find new ways to use workers regardless of age. The fact that this generation will be the healthiest and most vital group of older workers in history may also alter views about changing careers later in life and about how long people should work.[3]

4. **The workforce is showing greater ethnic diversity.** The percentage of all minority ethnic groups in the population will increase by the year 2005, and this increase will be reflected in the workforce. African Americans will make up 12 percent of the workforce; Hispanic Americans, 7.5 percent; Asians, 2.6 percent; and Native Americans, .8 percent. Together, these groups will represent almost one in four workers. Companies have responded to this trend by creating ethnic diversity programs to help workers understand and appreciate cultural differences. This mix of cultures in the workplace will bring new perspectives to solving business problems, and you will be a more effective (and valuable) employee if you can work in a diverse workforce.

The workforce of the future will represent a broad range of gender, age, and ethnic differences. It's important for people entering the workforce to be aware of these changes and of the need to work with all different kinds of people. Learning to appreciate differences isn't just a nicety anymore, it's a workplace necessity.

What Does Your Workplace Look Like?

Following are descriptions of people in the workforce. Check all of the boxes that apply to people you currently work with. In the line after each group, put the number of people in your workplace who fall into that category.

Age:

❑ 14 to 15 years old _____

❑ 16 to 19 years old _____

❑ 20 to 24 years old _____

❑ 25 to 34 years old _____

❑ 35 to 44 years old _____

❑ 45 to 54 years old _____

❑ 55 to 64 years old _____

❑ 65 and over _____

Gender:

❑ Male _____

❑ Female _____

Ethnic Group:

❑ White _____
   (non-Hispanic origin)

❑ Black _____

❑ Hispanic origin _____

❑ Asian _____

❑ Native American _____

How would you rate diversity in your workplace?

❑ Low   ❑ Medium   ❑ High

Organizations and Work

In the U.S. economy, most workers—79 percent, in fact—are employed by service-producing organizations.[4] Service organizations include a wide variety of businesses—not just fast food franchises, which is the first thought many people have when they hear the words "service economy"—as shown in the following table. The type of organization is listed in the first column of the table. The second column shows the percentage of workers employed by each sector in 1994. The third column shows the projected employment in 2005.

Type of Organization	1994 Employment	2005 Employment
Transportation, communications, utilities	5.3%	4.9%
Wholesale trade	5.4%	5%
Retail trade	18%	17.7%
Finance, insurance, and real estate	6.15%	5.7%
Services	27.2%	32.9%
Government	16.9%	16.1%

The remaining portion of the workforce (the other 21 percent) is employed in goods-producing organizations. This sector of the economy has had a declining share of employment for the past several decades, and continued decline is expected. The table below shows current and projected employment for these businesses.

Type of Business	1994 Employment	2005 Employment
Mining	.5%	.3%
Construction	4.4	4.2
Manufacturing	16.1	13.1

A decline in an industry doesn't mean you can't find a good job in that sector. But working in an industry with declining employment means you must continuously develop your skills. And, to be safe, you also should develop skills that will help you get a job in another industry if you have to. This is a lesson many people learned as a result of corporate restructuring in the past several years.

Not only are most workers employed in service-producing fields, 84 percent are working for smaller (1,000 or less employees) organizations. In fact, 66 percent of workers in the United States are employed by organizations with 250 or fewer employees. And, smaller organizations are less likely than larger ones to provide their workers with training.[5] This means most workers must assess their own training needs and take control of their training and education. In other words, you are responsible for your own employability and competitiveness in today's workforce.

What Kind of Organization Do You Work For?

Do you work for a service-producing or a goods-producing organization? _____

_____

_____

How big is the organization you work for? _____

_____

What skills do people need to work in this organization? _____

_____

_____

What skills do people need to advance in this organization? _____

_____

_____

What other industries interest you? _____

_____

What skills do you have that can be used in other organizations?

_____

_____

Occupational Trends

The fastest growing jobs in the labor market fall primarily into two categories, examples of which can be found in the 15 occupations with the largest projected number of job openings from 1994 to 2005.[6] Jobs in the first category require little education and typically are low-paying: for example, cashiers, janitors, waiters, home health aides, guards, and nursing aides. Jobs in the second require more education and typically have higher pay: for example, general managers, executives, systems analysts, registered nurses, teachers, and marketing supervisors.

This occupational trend helps explain why a person's level of education has such a dramatic affect on their earnings.[7] The following table illustrates the relationship between education and earnings. The third column shows the percentage of difference in average earnings over the earnings of a high school graduate.

Level of Education	Avg. Monthly Earnings	Difference
No high school diploma	$508	N/A
High school diploma	$1,080	0
Vocational certificate	$1,303	21%
Some college, no degree	$1,375	27%
College degree	$2,339	117%
Advanced degree	$3,331	208%
Professional degree	$5,067	369%

The difference in earnings over a lifetime is staggering. Let's assume that a high school graduate begins working full-time when he is 18 and retires 47 years later, at age 65. His total life earnings would be about $609,000. The college graduate who begins working at age 23 and retires at age 65 works for 42 years, but earns about $1,178,856. Earnings and employment opportunities for less educated workers declined significantly in the last decade, and that trend is likely to increase in the future.[8] There's truth to the old adage, education pays.

It's also important—in fact, in today's economy, it's necessary—to continue learning once you're on the job.[9] While many businesses provide training, it's up to you to take charge of your continuing education. (We'll look at this in Chapter 6.)

Thinking About Your Education

What education is required for your job? _____

How much do you earn a month? (If you're not sure, multiply your hourly wage by 173 if you work full-time, or by the number of hours you work in an average month if you work part-time.) _____

How do your education and earnings compare with the national average for your occupation? (You can find this information in the *Occupational Outlook Handbook [OOH]*.[10]) _____

Are you planning to get a job in another occupation? _____

What are the educational requirements and average earnings for this occupation? (Again, you can find this information in the *OOH*.)

_____

What kind of training does your current job offer? _____

_____

How can this training help you advance in your current job? _____

_____

_____

How can the training help prepare you for a future occupation? _____

_____

_____

Write down some ways you can keep your education current and get the skills you need to be successful. _____

_____

_____

The Structure of Work

The structure of work is changing, and that affects the way jobs are organized. Most organizations recognize the need to have a flexible workforce. This flexibility allows a business to keep its workforce as small as possible, thus saving money. This means that a great deal of work is now organized into projects, which are then contracted out to workers. These workers are hired to complete a specific project, at the end of which, their contract with the business ends. The changing nature of work has been documented by several experts.[11]

Workers typically fall into one of three categories: core employees, subcontractors, and temporary hires.

■ **Core employees** are those hired by
an organization to work full-time on
an ongoing basis. These are
employees who have some loyalty to
the organization and who
understand both its short-term and
its long-term goals. They usually are
provided with benefits like vacation
time, holiday pay, and health
insurance. Core employees are
workers who hold what we
traditionally call *permanent jobs*.
Core employees often coordinate or
lead projects for an organization, and
their work is supplemented by
subcontractors and temporary
employees.

Key Definition

Contingent Workforce

The *contingent workforce* refers to individuals who fall into one of the following categories: part-time workers, self-employed people working as independent contractors for organizations, workers hired for temporary periods of time, and workers who are employed through temporary employment firms. It is estimated that contingent workers make up 25 percent of the workforce.

■ **Subcontractors** are private business
owners—including self-employed
individuals—who provide services to
an organization, such as cleaning,
maintenance, payroll, accounting, security, computer programming,
telecommunications, and printing. Subcontractors or their employees
typically are paid a fee for completion of a task rather than a wage. Their
services may be used for a specific project and their work ends when the
project is completed. It is estimated that 1 in 11 workers in the United
States is self-employed.[12] Many workers who have lost jobs to corporate
restructuring in recent years have become self-employed.

■ **Temporary workers** are those who are hired by an organization for a
short time or whose services are obtained through a temporary
employment service. Many organizations prefer to use a "temp service"
because it reduces their paperwork, administrative tasks, and recruitment
efforts. Temporary workers may be hired to work on a specific project,
and their employment ends when the project is completed. Temporary
workers also are hired when the work load increases beyond the capacity
of core employees, in which case, there may be no specific date when
the work is completed. Rather, the organization stops using the workers'
services when the work load decreases. Temporary employees often do
not have fringe benefits—unless they are provided by the temp service—
and their work can be terminated with no advance notice.

So, what does all this mean for you? It means *you are responsible for your own career*. In today's economy, you simply cannot rely on an employer to provide a job. When one job ends, you must be prepared to find another. It's important to develop as many skills as possible, so that you can adapt to new tasks and projects, and to be prepared to work as a core employee or as a contingent worker. Adaptability and a willingness to work in any structure allows you to take charge of your own career.

Applying What You've Learned

Alisha is a computer repair technician for a company with about 100 employees. She is paid by a temporary service firm. Alisha earned her associate degree from a community college three years ago. She earns about $600 a week but has no fringe benefits.

1. What kind of worker is Alisha? _____

_____

2. If you were Alisha, would you continue to work for this company? Give a reason for your answer._____

_____

_____

3. What could Alisha do to increase her opportunities to work as a core employee? _____

_____

_____

Jamal is an orderly in a hospital. He is employed full-time and receives several fringe benefits, such as paid holidays, paid vacation time, and health insurance. He earns about $350 per week. Jamal enjoys working in a medical environment but thinks he needs to earn more money. He graduated from high school, but he didn't like school and he doesn't want to go to college.

1. What kind of worker is Jamal?_____

_____

_____

2. Would you be satisfied working in this situation? Explain your answer. _____

_____

_____

3. What do you think Jamal could do to improve his salary and his work situation? _____

_____

_____

Herschel is self-employed, which means he pays for all of his own fringe benefits. He spends most of his time working for a large corporation. He processes payroll checks for the company's employees, keeps time records, and files employment tax reports. Herschel has a bachelor's degree in accounting. His business earns about $40,000 a year, but he would like to earn much more money.

1. What kind of worker is Herschel? _____

_____

_____

2. Would you be satisfied with a work situation like Herschel's? _____

_____

_____

3. What do you think Herschel can do to make more money? _____

_____

_____

Summing Up

In today's changing workplace, the keyword is flexibility. As the economy continues to shift from goods-producing to services-producing, new and different skills are needed. And as companies rely more on subcontractors and temporary workers, finding new ways to offer your skills (and learning new skills to offer!) is crucial to your long-term success. Whether dealing with people from different cultural backgrounds or finding new ways to put your skills to work, the more flexible you are, the better your chances of success will be.

Notes

1. Howard N. Fullerton, Jr., "The 2005 Labor Force: Growing, But Slowly," *Monthly Labor Review* (November 1995), 29-44.

2. U.S. Department of Labor, *Report on the American Workforce* (Washington, DC: Government Printing Office, 1994).

3. Gail Sheehy, *New Passages: Mapping Your Life Across Time* (New York: Random House, 1995).

4. Ronald E. Kutscher, "Summary of BLS Projection to 2005," *Monthly Labor Review* (November 1995), 3-9.

5. Harley J. Frazis, Diane E. Herz, and Michael W. Harrigan, "Employer-Provided Training: Results from a New Survey," *Monthly Labor Review* (May 1995), 3-17.

6. George T. Silvestri, "Occupational Employment to 2005," *Monthly Labor Review* (November 1995), 60-84.

7. Rosalind R. Bruno, "What's It Worth? Field of Training and Economic Status: 1993," *Current Population Reports*, U.S. Census Bureau (December 1995).

8. U.S. Department of Labor, *Report on the American Workforce* (Washington, DC: Government Printing Office, 1994).

9. Derwin Fox, "Career Insurance for Today's World," *Training & Development* (March 1996), 61-64.

10. U.S. Department of Labor, *Occupational Outlook Handbook* (Indianapolis: JIST, 1996).

11. William Bridges, *Jobshift: How to Prosper in a Workplace Without Jobs* (New York: Addison-Wesley, 1994).

12. John E. Bregger, "Measuring Self-Employment in the United States," *Monthly Labor Review* (January/February 1995), 3-9.

Chapter 2

Your Employment Relationship

Whenever you start a new adventure, you have expectations about what will happen. Starting a new job is one such adventure. You may expect the job to be the start of a highly successful career, or you may simply expect it to help pay for a new car. Research shows that the more realistic your expectations are about a job, the more likely it is you will enjoy it.[1] In this chapter, we'll look at what employers expect from their employees, and what you should expect from your employer.

What Does My Employer Want, Anyway?

There's an old saying that goes like this: If you want to understand someone, you've got to walk a mile in their shoes. Suppose for a minute that you are the proud owner of a restaurant. Now answer these questions.

1. What are some important things that your business must do to run productively and efficiently?

2. What skills do you want your employees to have?

Now compare your answer to question 2 with those found in the study described below.

Workplace Basics

The U.S. Secretary of Labor created a commission to "define the know-how needed in the workplace." The Secretary's Commission on Achieving Necessary Skills (SCANS) was made up of people from business, education, and government, who identified the skills that are needed to succeed in high-skilled, high-paid jobs. They listed three foundational skills and five workplace competencies.[2] The foundation skills include:

1. **Basic skills**, including reading, writing, mathematics, speaking, and listening.

2. **Thinking skills**, including the ability to learn, reason, think creatively, make decisions, and solve problems.

3. **Personal qualities**, including individual responsibility, self-esteem, self-management, sociability, and integrity.

Workplace competencies are those skills needed for workers to be productive. The commission listed five of these:

1. **Resources**, including the ability to allocate time, money, materials, space, and staff.

2. **Interpersonal skills**, including the ability to work on teams, teach others, serve customers, lead, negotiate, and work with people from diverse cultural backgrounds.

3. **Information**, including the ability to acquire and evaluate data, organize and maintain files, interpret and communicate, and use computers to process information.

4. **Systems,** including the ability to understand social, organizational, and technological systems; monitor and correct performance; and design or improve systems.

5. **Technology**, including the ability to select equipment and tools, apply technology to specific tasks, and maintain and troubleshoot equipment.

The SCANS report demonstrates an important fact: Different, higher-level skills are needed in today's labor market than were required 20 years ago. This report is supported by the *Workplace Basics* study conducted by the American Society for Training and Development (ASTD).[3]

The ASTD asked employers throughout the United States what basic skills their employees need. The study found that most employers want their employees to possess *the workplace basics*, including these:

1. **Knowing how to learn.** The concept of lifelong learning is common in the business community. Employers spent approximately *$60 billion* in 1996 on formal employee training.[4] In 1985, U.S. businesses spent an estimated *$180 billion* for informal or on-the-job training.[5] Employees who don't have good learning skills will be unable to take advantage of this investment and may soon find their skills obsolete.

2. **Reading, writing, and computation.** People who are weak in these skills will have trouble in most jobs. The Hudson Institute has predicted that the average education required for a job by the year 2000 will be 13.5 years, compared with the current level of 12.8 years.[6]

3. **Listening and oral communication.** "The average person spends 8.4 percent of communications time writing, 13.3 percent reading, 23 percent speaking, and 55 percent listening."[7] Communication is as critical to success on the job as the three Rs.

4. **Adaptability.** Organizations must be flexible to adapt and keep pace with advances in technology, changes in the marketplace, and new management practices. Employees who are creative problem-solvers are essential to today's businesses.

5. **Personal management.** This category covers self-esteem, goal-setting and motivation, and personal and career development. For businesses to

succeed, employees must take pride in their work and be able to formulate and achieve goals. Finally, employees must know how to advance within an organization, and how to transfer skills to another business. As more businesses engage in participative management, these skills will become increasingly necessary.

6. **Group effectiveness.** Individualism is a thing of the past in most jobs. It is far more important that workers understand and practice teamwork, negotiation, and interpersonal skills. People who understand how to work effectively in groups are the foundations of successful enterprises.

7. **Influence.** Each employee must establish his or her own influence in order to successfully contribute ideas to an organization. Employees must understand the organizational structure and informal networks in order to implement new ideas or to complete some tasks.

Skills Checklist

Look at the following checklist and rank in order from 1 (most important) to 10 (least important) the employee skills that are most important to the success of your organization.

Work habits	_____
Dependability	_____
Desire to get ahead	_____
Quality of work	_____
Concern for productivity	_____
Responsibility	_____
Ability to read and apply printed matter	_____
Attitudes toward company and employer	_____
Ability to follow instructions	_____
Ability to write and speak effectively	_____

Key Definition

Dependability vs. Responsibility

The dictionary definitions of these words are similar. But when we use them in the world of work, they have slightly different meanings. *Dependability* means being on time and at work every day and notifying your supervisor when you are unable to be there. *Reliability* means following through with a job. When the boss asks you to do a job, you get it done, and you look for things to do when you have completed assigned tasks.

Skills Examples

Listed below are the same skills you ranked earlier. In the spaces below, explain why each is important in making an organization work. Give an example of how each skill is used in the workplace.

Work habits _____

_____

_____

Dependability _____

_____

_____

Desire to get ahead _____

_____

_____

Quality of work _____

_____

_____

Concern for productivity _____

_____

_____

Responsibility _____

_____

_____

Ability to read and apply printed matter _____

_____

_____

Attitudes toward company and employer _____

_____

_____

Ability to follow instructions _____

_____

_____

Ability to write and speak effectively _____

_____

_____

In the first exercise, you listed those things an employer needs to run a productive and efficient organization. Three essentials you might have included on your list are these:

1. **Provide a product or service of high quality.** Consumers want quality in whatever they buy. Organizations today place great emphasis on quality. The U.S. government even recognizes companies for their emphasis on quality with the Malcolm Baldridge National Quality Award.[8]

2. **Satisfy the customer's needs and wants.** An organization depends on the good will of its customers. If customers are pleased with products purchased or services received, they will continue to do business with an organization and even recommend it to friends. Conversely, a bad experience will be talked about with friends, family members, acquaintances, coworkers, and complete strangers.

3. Make a profit. Product quality and customer satisfaction have to be provided at a cost that allows a business to make a profit. There's no reason for the owners or stockholders to continue the business if they could invest their money elsewhere and receive a higher rate of return.

An employer expects all employees to help the organization accomplish the three essentials of a successful operation. Employees are expected to work hard, help when asked, please customers, and do it for a wage that allows the organization to make a profit and stay in business.

Employee Skills

Employers want employees who have more than just the skills needed to do a specific job. They look for employees with a broader base of skills: These are called adaptive or self-management skills, and they help employees adjust to the workplace. For example, getting along with coworkers and listening to a supervisor's instructions are adaptive skills. These skills will be explored more fully in Chapter 7.

In 1975, the Advisory Council for Technical-Vocational Education in Texas compiled a list of skills surveyed employers wanted in their employees.[9] (Other surveys in the past two decades have supported their findings.[10]) In the survey, employers were asked to identify areas in which their employees needed to improve. The order in which employers ranked 10 items is shown below.

Key Definition

Profit

The money an organization earns through sales or services is *income*. All bills the organization pays are *expenses*. *Profit* is the amount of money an organization has left after paying all its expenses. Profits belong to the owner, partners, or stockholders of an organization; profit is the compensation business owners receive for risking their money in a commercial venture. Often owners take money from their profit and reinvest it in the organization by buying new equipment, opening new facilities, or hiring new workers. This creates a healthy economy. Some business owners have profit-sharing programs that distribute a share of profits to all employees as a reward for their hard work.

Even government and nonprofit agencies must stay within a budget. Nonprofit agencies must earn enough money to pay all their expenses. Although they can't distribute earnings greater than their expenses to stock-holders, government and nonprofit agencies are expected to operate as efficiently as profit-making businesses.

Skills Employers Want in Their Employees

1. Concern for productivity
2. Pride of craftsmanship and quality of work
3. Responsibility and ability to follow through on assigned tasks
4. Dependability
5. Good work habits
6. Positive attitudes toward company and employer
7. Ability to write and speak effectively
8. Ability to read and apply printed matter
9. Ability to follow instructions
10. Ambition/motivation/desire to get ahead

Ask yourself how many of these skills you have demonstrated in the past. Think of ways you can practice these skills on the job. Remember, your employer hired you for your skills, and your value in the company increases when you apply these skills on the job.

Applying What You've Learned

Tom takes orders at a fast-food restaurant. He has worked at the restaurant for three weeks and believes he deserves a raise. After his shift, Tom talks with his supervisor, Janet, and tells her that he feels he deserves a raise.

1. If you were Janet, what would you tell Tom? _____

_____

_____

2. Why? _____

_____

_____

You are a supervisor in a large insurance company. This morning, you asked a file clerk named Angel to go to the supply room for a box of new file folders. Later, you found Angel sitting at her desk, filing her nails. When you asked, "Why aren't you working?" Angel replied, "I ran out of file folders."

1. What would you say to Angel? _____

   _____

   _____

2. What skill(s) does she need to improve? _____

   _____

   _____

What Should You Expect?

Most of us have several reasons for working. Your motivation and interest in a job depend on your reasons for working and how well the job satisfies your needs.

1. List your reasons for working. You may think of money first. That's fine, but also think of the other reasons you work.

   _____

   _____

   _____

2. Think about the jobs you've had. What did you like about each job? What did you dislike?

   _____

   _____

   _____

3. How do you expect an employer to treat you? What are things you want in return for the work you do?

   _____

   _____

   _____

Reasons for Working

You can't expect every job to satisfy all of your expectations and values. Many people work at jobs they don't want until they can get the education or experience necessary to start the career they do want. Sometimes it's necessary to make sacrifices while you work toward the job you want. You must determine your most important expectations and values, then evaluate what each job offers.

Many studies have asked what American workers consider their most important job values and expectations. A 1993 study, reported in *The Wall Street Journal*, asked people the reasons they considered "very important" in deciding to take their current jobs.[11] The reasons given by 50 percent or more of the people are shown below. (By the way, salary or wages were cited by only 35 percent.)

Reason Workers Like Their Work	Percentage of Workers
Open communication	65%
Effects on family/personal life	60
Nature of work	59
Management quality	59
Supervisor	58
Control over work content	55
Gain new skills	55
Job security	54
Coworker quality	53
Job location	50
Stimulating work	50

A 1995 survey reported in *HR Magazine* asked human resource professionals to rank the most pressing concerns of their employees.[12] Notice that the responses in this survey differ somewhat from the those in *The Wall Street Journal* survey. Two factors may account for the differences: (1) the first survey questioned employees, while the second questioned human resource managers; (2) the first survey asked about major concerns *before taking a job,* while the second reported concerns of employees *on the job.* Whatever the reason for the differences, it's important to note there are also similarities.

Items	Highest rank
Job security	1
Compensation	2
Benefit costs	3
Job satisfaction	4
Career advancement	5
Recognition	6
Dependent care	7
Work environment	8
Job training	9
Vacation time	10

In *Human Relations: A Job-Oriented Approach*, Andrew DuBrin suggested there are both external factors and internal causes that affect job satisfaction.[13] When you compare the lists below, you will see that there are fewer external factors controlled by the employer than are controlled by employees. To a large degree, *you* are responsible for the way you feel about your job. You can increase your job satisfaction by focusing on the internal causes and rewards of what you are doing.

External Factors

- Mentally challenging work
- Reasonable physical demands
- Meaningful rewards
- Contact with customer/end user
- Helpful coworkers and superiors

Internal Causes

- Interest in the work itself
- Work fitting one's job values
- Positive self-image
- Good personal adjustment
- Positive expectations about the job
- A feeling of self-esteem reinforced by the job optimism and flexibility

In addition to the things you expect from an employer, there are certain requirements the federal and state governments place on all employers. In the next section, we'll review these requirements.

Understanding Your Rights

There are several things the law requires an employer to do for employees, many of which are listed below. Keep in mind that these explanations are quite general. Labor law is continually changing as new laws are passed by federal and state governments. It's further complicated by court decisions as to how these laws should be interpreted.

If you think your employer isn't following the law, you should respectfully discuss this with your supervisor. If you aren't satisfied with the answers you get, then you may decide to contact an elected official, such as a state representative or senator, the mayor's office, or the governor's office to find out what organization you must contact to get your questions answered. Reporting these concerns may cause serious problems for your employer, so you should carefully consider the results of your action.

Federal Laws

There are a number of laws and regulations that affect workers on the job. Since it's difficult to provide a summary of all regulations for all 50 states, I have listed only the federal regulations for each topic.

Fair Wage

- **The Fair Labor Standards Act (FLSA)** governs the minimum wage, working hours, and child labor laws. The specifics of this law are changed frequently.

- **The Work Hours Act of 1962** extends the application of FLSA, including provisions for paying employees time-and-a-half.

- **The Equal Pay Act of 1972** established equal payment for overtime work, regardless of gender.

- **The Walsh-Healy Act** governs the minimum wage to be paid for federal government suppliers of equipment, materials, and supplies.

- **The Davis-Bacon Act** governs the minimum wage to be paid by contractors for federally funded construction projects.

Most employers are required to pay workers at least the minimum wage. It is estimated that almost 92 percent of all employers must pay the minimum wage. This wage varies according to federal regulations. Some states have minimum wage laws that require employers to pay a higher wage than the federal minimum. In a few cases, counties and cities have established minimum wage laws.

1. What is the minimum wage in your state? _____

_____

2. What is the current federal minimum wage? _____

_____

3. Does your county or city have a minimum wage law? If so, what is the current minimum wage? _____

_____

Equal Opportunity

■ **The Age Discrimination in Employment Act of 1967** prohibits firms with 20 or more employees from discriminating against workers 40 years of age and older.

■ **The Equal Employment Opportunity Act of 1972** prohibits firms with 20 or more employees from discriminating against workers because of their race, gender, religion, or national origin.

■ **The Pregnancy Discrimination Act of 1978** requires that pregnant women be entitled to benefits related to sick leave that would be given for other medical reasons.

■ **The Vocational Rehabilitation Act of 1973** prohibits employers with federal contracts of $2,500 or greater from discriminating against persons because of physical or mental impairments.

■ **The Vietnam-Era Veterans' Readjustment Act of 1974** prohibits firms with federal contracts of $10,000 or more from discriminating against Vietnam-era veterans.

■ **The Americans with Disabilities Act** prohibits employers from discriminating against workers because of physical or mental disabilities.

Your employer cannot discriminate in pay, promotions, training, or in any other way because of your race, gender, age, disability, national origin, or religion.

How would you pursue a question about discrimination? _____

_____

_____

Child Labor Laws

Employers are expected to abide by child labor laws. These laws prevent businesses from employing anyone under the age of 14. Workers ages 14 and 15 are limited in the number of hours and the time of day they can work, and are excluded from work in manufacturing, mining, or hazardous jobs. Workers ages 16 and 17 also are excluded from employment in hazardous jobs. Employers are responsible for obtaining proof of age from the young people they hire. This is the reason many employers ask for a work permit. High school counselors can advise students about how to obtain a work permit.

Are you under 18? If so, what restrictions will you have because of your age? _____

_____

_____

_____

Worker Safety

■ **The Occupational Safety and Health Act of 1970 (OSHA)** places several requirements on employers to provide safe working conditions for employees and protects from dismissal employees who report unsafe working conditions.

- **The Hazard Communication Standard** (an addition to OSHA) prescribes a system for informing employees about health hazards and how to respond to exposure from such hazards.

There are many federal and state laws governing employee safety. Employers are expected to provide a work area that is both safe and clean. Equipment must have protective guards. Employers must make sure employees wear proper safety equipment such as eye protectors, hard hats, or steel-toed shoes. Employees also should be informed about any hazardous materials they may work with, as well as what to do in case they are exposed to hazardous materials. Again, youth under 18 years of age are restricted from working in any hazardous occupation.

What organization in your state reviews safety conditions in the workplace? _____

_____

_____

Labor Relations

- **The Wagner Act of 1935** guarantees employees the right to organize and participate in union activities.

- **The Taft-Hartley Act of 1947** balances the rights of employers and unions.

- **The Landrum-Griffin Act of 1957** guarantees union members certain rights within the union itself.

Employers are required by federal and some state laws to allow employees to participate in lawful union activity, but some employers may try to find another way to fire you for such participation. Carefully check with other employees to find out what they see as the benefits and drawbacks of joining a local union.

Several states also have right-to-work laws, which ensure that you aren't *required* to join a union that exists at your workplace. However, if you live in a state without this provision, you may be required to pay union dues even if you don't join, because you benefit from the collective bargaining. Union dues vary and are usually handled as automatic deductions from paychecks.

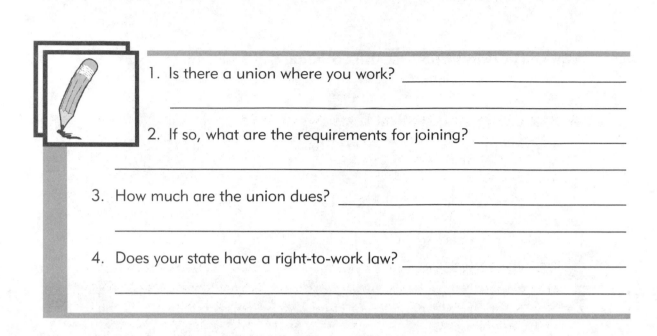

1. Is there a union where you work? _____
    _____

2. If so, what are the requirements for joining? _____
    _____

3. How much are the union dues? _____
    _____

4. Does your state have a right-to-work law? _____
    _____

Fair Treatment

■ **The Worker Adjustment and Retraining Notification Act (WARN)**
requires employers to provide 60 days advance warning for major layoffs
or plant closings. The law covers only certain employers.[14]

Employment-at-will is a legal term that means an employer can fire you at
any time for any reason, but the termination cannot be in violation of federal
or state law. The application of this law has been changed over the years by
many state courts and some state legislatures. The *wrongful discharge* concept has diminished the application of employment-at-will: This concept says
that an employee should be dismissed only for *just cause*, which places the
burden of proof on the employer to show that the employee has done something serious enough to justify termination. The law related to dismissals
varies from state to state and is undergoing a great deal of change. The only
way a worker can be sure he or she was unfairly dismissed is to obtain the
services of an attorney, which is often prohibitively expensive and time-
consuming.

What are the laws in your state that apply to the dismissal of an
employee? _____
_____
_____
_____

Working Conditions

- **The Family and Medical Leave Act of 1993** covers organizations with 50 or more employees and applies to employees who have worked for the organization at least one year and for at least 1,250 hours in the 12 months before the leave is requested. The law requires that employers give employees unpaid leaves for up to 12 weeks for family and medical reasons. An employee given this leave must be allowed to return to the same job or a similar one.

- **The Civil Rights Act of 1964** prohibits sexual harassment, including unwelcome sexual advances, requests for sexual favors, and verbal or physical conduct of a sexual nature that creates a hostile or abusive work environment. Some states have passed laws defining and prohibiting sexual harassment.

1. Does your employer qualify for the Family and Medical Leave Act? Do you personally qualify? _____

_____

2. Does your state have a law against sexual harassment? Summarize the law.

_____

Resolving Employee Rights Issues

It's important to know your rights as an employee. It's also important to remember that some employers are not familiar with these laws or do not strictly follow them. You must determine for yourself how important a problem is before you discuss it with your supervisor. Employees who constantly question possible violations of laws, policies, and procedures may be viewed as troublemakers. If the problem is serious and you do decide to pursue the matter, follow the guidelines below.

1. **Discuss the problem with your supervisor and ask him or her to correct the situation.** Approach the conversation in a calm and respectful manner. Keep in mind that you may not correctly understand the situation. Give your supervisor an opportunity to explain why the problem may not be as serious as you think.

2. **If the supervisor doesn't correct the problem or you feel the explanation is inadequate, contact the personnel office or the owner.** (Personnel handbooks usually describe the process you should follow when appealing a supervisor's actions.) Discuss your concerns and how they can be satisfied. Always do this in a polite and nonthreatening manner. Be aware that your relationship with your supervisor may be negatively affected by this action.

3. **If the company doesn't correct the problem, you can contact the government agency responsible for seeing that the law is enforced.** Your employer may fire you for this unless a specific law protects you from such an action.

When you approach a government agency to file a complaint, you'll find that the follow-through requires a great deal of your time. You must meet with government officials to explain the problem. You may be required to testify at formal hearings. It's important to balance out the time requirements and pressures that are part of such formal complaints against the benefits of having an employer change its illegal practices.

Applying What You've Learned

Kim works for a manufacturing company. The wages are not as high as those at similar companies in the area. The other workers are friendly and helpful. When someone has a problem, everyone helps out. The supervisor is a hard worker and pushes everyone to produce a high-quality product as quickly as possible. The supervisor is easy to talk to and will listen to questions and complaints from employees. Kim is often asked to work overtime. It is not unusual for her to work six days a week.

1. What is positive in Kim's situation? _____

_____

2. What is negative? _____

_____

3. How likely would you be to continue working at this job? _____

_____

Jackson is a hospital nurse. The pay and benefits are good, but the hospital often changes procedures without informing the staff first. Sometimes, Jackson doesn't find out about changes until they are to be put into practice. Jackson reports to a supervisor who is not very friendly. Other workers are cooperative, but they do not get together outside of work.

1. What is positive in Jackson's situation? _____

_____

2. What is negative? _____

_____

3. How likely would you be to continue working at this job? _____

_____

Summing Up

Your relationship with an employer is built upon three important concepts:

1. You must understand that the employer is in business to make a profit—not just to provide you with a job.

2. If you understand why you want to work, and look for things in your job that satisfy your reasons for working, you will be happier and do a better job.

3. It's important to maintain a relationship of mutual respect with your employer. The employer may be required by law to behave toward you in a certain way. Many employers want to do much more. You should respect the employer's reasons for policies and decisions that affect you. Always try to resolve misunderstandings in a positive manner.

Notes

1. G. Leveto and J. Aplin, "Individual Expectation: Relationships to Attitudes, Perceptions, and Intent to Turnover," *Proceedings of the 21st Annual Meeting of the Midwest Academy of Management* (1978), 134.

2. The Secretary's Commission on Achieving Necessary Skills, U.S. Department of Labor, *Learning a Living: A Blueprint for High Performance, a SCANS Report for America 2000* (Washington, DC: Government Printing Office, 1992).

3. Anthony P. Carnevale, Leila J. Gainer, and Ann S. Meltzer, *Workplace Basics: The Skills Employers Want,* conducted by the American Society for Training and Development (Washington, DC: Department of Labor, 1988).

4. "1996 Industry Report," *Training* (October 1996), 37.

5. *Serving The New Corporation,* (Alexandria, VA, American Society for Training and Development, 1986).

6. William B. Johnson and Arnold H. Packer, *Workforce 2000,* (Indianapolis, IN: The Hudson Institute, 1987).

7. Inid 3

8. Patricia A. Galagan, "David T. Kearns: A CEO's View of Training," *Training and Development Journal, 44*(5), 41.

9. The Advisory Council for Technical-Vocational Education in Texas, *Qualities Employers Like and Dislike in Job Applicants: Final Report of Statewide Employer Survey* (Austin: 1975).

10. Norma DeMario, "Skills Needed for Successful Employment: A Review of the Literature, *RE:view* (September 1, 1992), 115.

11. Sue Shellenbarger, "Work-Force Study Finds Loyalty Is Weak, Divisions of Race and Gender Are Deep," *The Wall Street Journal* (September 3, 1993), B1.

12. Michelle Neely Martinez, "Job Security No. 1 Employee Concern," *HR Magazine,* (Decmber, 1995), 16.

13. Andrew J. Dubrin, *Human Relations: A Job-Oriented Approach,* (Englewood Cliffs, NJ: Prentice-Hall, 1988), 74.

14. Fred S. Steingold, *The Employer's Legal Handbook,* (Berkeley, CA: Nolo Press, 1994), 11.

Chapter 3

Avoiding the
New Job Blues

The impression you make on your supervisor and coworkers your first day on the job has an effect on your future relationship with them. The first day can be confusing and difficult, because you have a great deal to remember; and this confusion can make it tough to create a positive first impression. But you can reduce the confusion by knowing what to expect on the first day and being prepared.

The first day on a job obviously will differ from one organization to another, but some things are the same. Here are some typical first day activities in most organizations.

- **Reporting to work.** In large organizations, you probably will report to the personnel or human resources office. Smaller companies may have you report to the office manager or directly to your new supervisor.

- **Orientation.** Organizations with more than 100 employees usually provide some kind of orientation training for new employees to introduce them to the organization, take care of necessary paperwork, and review policies and benefits.[1]

- **Job introduction and tour.** You usually will receive an introduction to the job you have been hired to do. This often is conducted by the supervisor. Frequently your supervisor also will show you around the work area and other parts of the facility. During this tour you will be introduced to people you need to know.

In this chapter we'll review what to expect from each of these activities.

Reporting to Work

You must be prepared to make a good impression the first day on the job. Contacting your new supervisor a day or two before you are scheduled to start helps make the transition to the new job easier. Ask him or her about anything that requires your attention before you arrive at your new job. You might ask these questions:

- What is appropriate clothing to wear for this job?

- When I arrive, where should I go and whom should I contact?

- Should I bring identification or any other documents?

- Are there tools, equipment, or other items that I am expected to furnish?

The next section contains some checklists to help you prepare for your first day at work. Get the information you need to complete the checklists by asking the personnel department or your supervisor.

Dress Appropriately

It's embarrassing to show up for work dressed the wrong way. You stand out like a sore thumb and people remember you for weeks (or even months) because of how you looked that first day. You should ask your supervisor what type of clothing is suitable or required for the job. Think about any special dress situations that may be necessary for your job.

Are there any special clothing requirements your employer may have?_____

_____

_____

_____

Your employer may require you to wear a uniform. If so, find out if it is issued on your first day or if you are to arrive in uniform on the first day. You also should ask if you are expected to buy the uniform or if the company provides it.

Certain jobs require special safety clothing. Working with chemicals demands a variety of clothing, depending on how toxic the chemicals are. Hard hats and steel-toed safety shoes are required on some jobs to avoid injury. Working near machinery may require you to avoid wearing jewelry or loose clothing that could get caught in mechanical parts. Be aware of your organization's safety requirements and obey them.

Organizations for which no special clothing is required still have expectations about the way you dress. When you visit an organization for interviews, notice how the workers dress. After you are hired, ask your supervisor to advise you about what is appropriate to wear on your first day at work.

Dress Checklist

Examine this dress checklist. Pay special attention to the items you may need to wear on your first day.

Uniform

❏ Does employer provide uniform? _____

❏ When do I need it? _____

❏ Where do I pick it up? _____

❏ What items make up the uniform? _____

❏ How many of each item do I receive? _____

❏ What are my responsibilities for care and for returning the uniform when I leave the job? _____

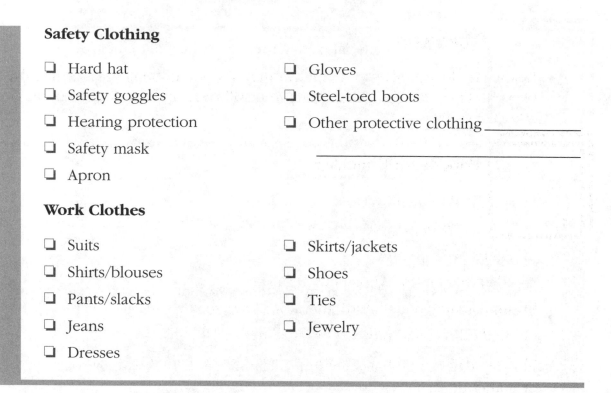

Safety Clothing

- ❏ Hard hat
- ❏ Safety goggles
- ❏ Hearing protection
- ❏ Safety mask
- ❏ Apron

- ❏ Gloves
- ❏ Steel-toed boots
- ❏ Other protective clothing _____
  _____

Work Clothes

- ❏ Suits
- ❏ Shirts/blouses
- ❏ Pants/slacks
- ❏ Jeans
- ❏ Dresses

- ❏ Skirts/jackets
- ❏ Shoes
- ❏ Ties
- ❏ Jewelry

Starting the Day

Talk with your supervisor or the personnel department before your first day on the job and ask exactly when you are to arrive, where to go, and whom you should contact. At some companies, you report on the first work day at a different time and location than you do on other work days.

First Day Checklist

Check off each item as you answer the question.

- ❏ What time should I arrive?
- ❏ Where should I report?
- ❏ To whom should I report?
- ❏ What documentation should I bring?
- ❏ What special equipment do I need?
- ❏ What will I be expected to do?
- ❏ What do people usually do for lunch?

Paperwork

Below are documents your employer may ask you to bring on your first day of work. Find out which documents you will need and check them off as you collect them.

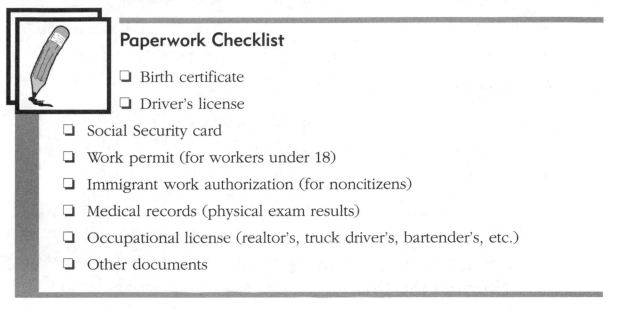

Paperwork Checklist

❑ Birth certificate

❑ Driver's license

❑ Social Security card

❑ Work permit (for workers under 18)

❑ Immigrant work authorization (for noncitizens)

❑ Medical records (physical exam results)

❑ Occupational license (realtor's, truck driver's, bartender's, etc.)

❑ Other documents

Orientation

Many employers conduct orientation training for new employees. In some organizations this is the responsibility of the personnel department, while in others it is done by the supervisor. Several important issues may be discussed during orientation, including these:

■ **Introduction.** You need to know what the organization does, how it is structured, and who the key people are.

■ **Payroll and personnel information.** You need to complete certain forms for payroll withholdings. You must also provide proof that you are a U.S. citizen. If you are an immigrant, you must prove that you can legally work in this country. Be prepared to provide this information when asked.

■ **Policies and practices review.** You should be informed about the important policies and practices of your employer. This includes information about vacations, holidays, and other days approved for excused absences.

■ **Benefits and services review.** You should have company benefits explained and be given a chance to discuss them.

■ **Employer expectation review.** You should be told what the employer expects. Many of the points reviewed in Chapter 2 will be discussed at this time.

The following section explains common benefits and personnel policies.[2] Though not all organizations offer the same benefits or follow the same procedures, the explanations here may help you more fully understand the orientation process.

Personnel Information

Most employers need certain documents to verify information about new employees. In most cases, you must provide these documents on or before your first day of work. This information frequently falls into four categories.

1. **Verification of citizenship/immigration.** Federal law requires employers to demonstrate that all workers are legally entitled to work in the United States. They must have proof of citizenship or an immigrant work authorization permit for each employee. A copy of your birth certificate usually is enough to document your citizenship.

2. **Social Security number.** This information is needed to withhold taxes.

3. **Licenses.** Some occupations require a license issued by the state government. If this is the case in your occupation, your employer will need to see the license and keep a copy for company records. The cost and license application is usually the worker's responsibility.

4. **Health forms.** Your employer may require you to have a physical exam. Most employers pay for the exam, and the results go directly to them. However, you may be asked to bring the results when you report in. The President's Commission on Organized Crime has recommended that all companies test employees for drug use.[3] Consequently, your employer may require you to take a drug test. If you are taking prescription medication, you should notify the people administering the drug test. If you test positive but have not been taking drugs, you should ask to be retested.

Applying What You've Learned

Chad arrived at Merlin Controls at 6:45 A.M., ready for his first day at work. He was stopped at the guard's gate from entering the plant because he didn't have an identification badge. Chad explained to the guard that it was his first day and gave her the name of his supervisor, Linda. The guard called Linda and asked Chad to wait until she came to escort him into the plant. Linda arrived at the gate 45 minutes later. She apologized for not coming sooner, but said she had problems to take care of first. Linda then told Chad he should report to the personnel office when it opened at 8 A.M. Chad waited in the reception area until the office opened.

1. How would you feel if you were Chad? _____

   _____

   _____

2. How could Chad have avoided this situation? _____

   _____

   _____

Felicia was excited about her first day as a claims processor trainee at Adams National Insurance Company, and she wanted to make a good first impression. She even took an early bus to make sure she arrived on time. When Felicia got to work, she was asked to show her Social Security card and driver's license for identification purposes. Felicia did not have them. The personnel officer told her that she could start training that day, but she would have to bring the documents tomorrow.

1. If you were Felicia, how would this make you feel?_____

   _____

   _____

2. How could Felicia have avoided this situation? _____

   _____

   _____

Payroll Information and Enrollment

Most employers will ask you to complete payroll information on your first day at work. This section explains what information your employer will require and why.

Withholding Taxes

There are three forms that typically must be completed by all new employees before they can be added to the payroll: a W-4 form for federal withholding taxes, a state tax withholding form, and an I-9 form to check citizenship and legal residence status. Your proof of citizenship or immigrant work authorization form will be used when you complete the I-9 form. The tax withholding forms are used for the following purposes:

- **Federal income taxes.** Federal income taxes will be automatically withheld from your paycheck by your employer. The amount of taxes withheld is based on the number of personal allowances you claim. You need to complete a W-4 form so your employer can calculate the correct tax to withhold.

- **State and local income taxes.** Most states and some cities and counties have income taxes. You must complete withholding forms for these taxes. Your employer uses the information you provide on the state withholding form to deduct the correct amount from your pay.

- **Federal Insurance Contributions Act (FICA).** This is a Social Security tax. A set percentage of your paycheck must be withheld by your employer, and your employer contributes a similar amount to your account. This money is used to fund retirement benefits and is credited to your personal account. Your account number is the same as your Social Security number.

Personal Allowances

The federal government lets you claim personal allowances for a variety of reasons. An allowance reduces the amount of money on which you pay taxes. You can claim an allowance for yourself, your spouse, and any dependents (children, elderly parents, etc.). In addition, special allowances are given if you are the head of a household, have childcare payments in excess of a specific amount each year, and for certain other reasons established by Congress.

Payroll Information

Typically, information is provided about payroll when you complete the payroll forms. You should check the following information.

■ **Method of payment.** Many companies now offer employees a choice of being paid by check or by direct deposit. A direct deposit places the money directly into your checking or savings account. You receive a form showing the amount of money your employer deposits. This saves you a trip to the bank to make the deposit yourself. The payroll department can give you details if your employer offers this service. You may still choose to receive an actual paycheck you can see and deposit yourself. But be prepared to tell your employer which method you prefer.

■ **Schedule of paydays.** Find out when you will receive your first paycheck. New employees are not always eligible for a paycheck on the first payday after they start work. You should also ask about the regular payday schedule. Some organizations only distribute paychecks at specific times. If your employer has such a policy and you are not scheduled to work during that time, you need to make arrangements to pick up your paycheck.

■ **Check your withholdings.** You can expect 15 percent or more of your check to be withheld for taxes and other deductions. Check the calculations for withholdings and deductions after you receive your first paycheck. If you don't understand how the calculations were made, talk to the payroll department. Below is a sample deduction form similar to that used by many employers.

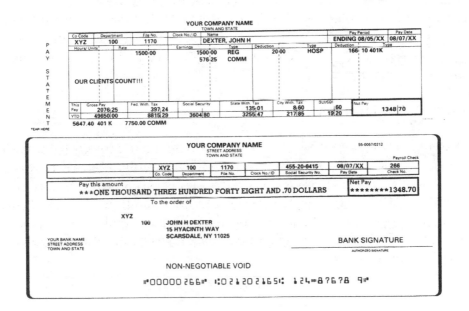

Applying What You've Learned

The following pages contain the Internal Revenue Service Form, or W-4, for 1996. The form changes slightly from one year to the next, but this sample will be useful for practice. Complete the form with the correct information for tax withholding.

Form W-4 (1996)

Want More Money In Your Paycheck?
If you expect to be able to take the earned income credit for 1996 and a child lives with you, you may be able to have part of the credit added to your take-home pay. For details, get Form W-5 from your employer.

Purpose. Complete Form W-4 so that your employer can withhold the correct amount of Federal income tax from your pay. Because your tax situation may change, you may want to refigure your withholding each year.

Exemption From Withholding. Read line 7 of the certificate below to see if you can claim exempt status. *If exempt, only complete lines 1, 2, 3, 4, 7, and sign the form to validate it.* No Federal income tax will be withheld from your pay. Your exemption expires February 18, 1997.

Note: *You cannot claim exemption from withholding if (1) your income exceeds $650*

and includes unearned income (e.g., interest and dividends) and (2) another person can claim you as a dependent on their tax return.
Basic Instructions. If you are not exempt, complete the Personal Allowances Worksheet. Additional worksheets are on page 2 so you can adjust your withholding allowances based on itemized deductions, adjustments to income, or two-earner/two-job situations. Complete all worksheets that apply to your situation. The worksheets will help you figure the number of withholding allowances you are entitled to claim. However, you may claim fewer allowances than this.

Head of Household. Generally, you may claim head of household filing status on your tax return only if you are unmarried and pay more than 50% of the costs of keeping up a home for yourself and your dependent(s) or other qualifying individuals.

Nonwage Income. If you have a large amount of nonwage income, such as interest or dividends, you should consider making estimated tax payments using Form 1040-ES.

Otherwise, you may find that you owe additional tax at the end of the year.
Two Earners/Two Jobs. If you have a working spouse or more than one job, figure the total number of allowances you are entitled to claim on all jobs using worksheets from only one W-4. This total should be divided among all jobs. Your withholding will usually be most accurate when all allowances are claimed on the W-4 filed for the highest paying job and zero allowances are claimed for the others.

Check Your Withholding. After your W-4 takes effect, use **Pub. 919**, Is My Withholding Correct for 1996?, to see how the dollar amount you are having withheld compares to your estimated total annual tax. Get Pub. 919 especially if you used the Two Earner/Two Job Worksheet and your earnings exceed $150,000 (Single) or $200,000 (Married). To order Pub. 919, call 1-800-829-3676. Check your telephone directory for the IRS assistance number for further help.

Sign This Form. Form W-4 is not considered valid unless you sign it.

Personal Allowances Worksheet

A Enter "1" for **yourself** if no one else can claim you as a dependent . . . . **A** _____

B Enter "1" if: {
- You are single and have only one job; or
- You are married, have only one job, and your spouse does not work; or
- Your wages from a second job or your spouse's wages (or the total of both) are $1,000 or less.
} **B** _____

C Enter "1" for your **spouse**. But, you may choose to enter -0- if you are married and have either a working spouse or more than one job (this may help you avoid having too little tax withheld) . . . . **C** _____

D Enter number of **dependents** (other than your spouse or yourself) you will claim on your tax return . . . . **D** _____

E Enter "1" if you will file as **head of household** on your tax return (see conditions under **Head of Household** above) . **E** _____

F Enter "1" if you have at least $1,500 of **child or dependent care expenses** for which you plan to claim a credit . . **F** _____

G Add lines A through F and enter total here. **Note:** This amount may be different from the number of exemptions you claim on your return ▶ **G** _____

For accuracy, do all worksheets that apply.
- If you plan to **itemize or claim adjustments to income** and want to reduce your withholding, see the Deductions and Adjustments Worksheet on page 2.
- If you are **single** and have **more than one job** and your combined earnings from all jobs exceed $30,000 OR if you are **married** and have a **working spouse or more than one job,** and the combined earnings from all jobs exceed $50,000, see the Two-Earner/Two-Job Worksheet on page 2 if you want to avoid having too little tax withheld.
- If **neither** of the above situations applies, **stop here** and enter the number from line G on line 5 of Form W-4 below.

------------------------ **Cut here and give the certificate to your employer. Keep the top portion for your records.** ------------------------

Form **W-4**	**Employee's Withholding Allowance Certificate**	OMB No. 1545-0010
Department of the Treasury Internal Revenue Service	▶ **For Privacy Act and Paperwork Reduction Act Notice, see reverse.**	19**96**

1 Type or print your first name and middle initial	Last name		**2** Your social security number

Home address (number and street or rural route)	**3** ☐ Single ☐ Married ☐ Married, but withhold at higher Single rate. **Note:** If married, but legally separated, or spouse is a nonresident alien, check the Single box.
City or town, state, and ZIP code	**4** If your last name differs from that on your social security card, check here and call 1-800-772-1213 for a new card . . . . . . ▶ ☐

5 Total number of allowances you are claiming (from line G above or from the worksheets on page 2 if they apply) . | **5** _____

6 Additional amount, if any, you want withheld from each paycheck . . . . | **6** $ _____

7 I claim exemption from withholding for 1996 and I certify that I meet **BOTH** of the following conditions for exemption:
- Last year I had a right to a refund of **ALL** Federal income tax withheld because I had **NO** tax liability; **AND**
- This year I expect a refund of **ALL** Federal income tax withheld because I expect to have **NO** tax liability.

If you meet both conditions, enter "EXEMPT" here . . . . ▶ | **7**

Under penalties of perjury, I certify that I am entitled to the number of withholding allowances claimed on this certificate or entitled to claim exempt status.

Employee's signature ▶ _____ Date ▶ _____ , 19___

8 Employer's name and address (Employer: Complete 8 and 10 only if sending to the IRS)	**9** Office code (optional)	**10** Employer identification number

Cat. No. 10220Q

Deductions and Adjustments Worksheet

Note: *Use this worksheet only if you plan to itemize deductions or claim adjustments to income on your 1996 tax return.*

1　Enter an estimate of your 1996 itemized deductions. These include qualifying home mortgage interest, charitable contributions, state and local taxes (but not sales taxes), medical expenses in excess of 7.5% of your income, and miscellaneous deductions. (For 1996, you may have to reduce your itemized deductions if your income is over $117,950 ($58,975 if married filing separately). Get Pub. 919 for details.)　**1** $ _____

2　Enter: { $6,700 if married filing jointly or qualifying widow(er)
$5,900 if head of household
$4,000 if single
$3,350 if married filing separately }　**2** $ _____

3　**Subtract** line 2 from line 1. If line 2 is greater than line 1, enter -0-　**3** $ _____

4　Enter an estimate of your 1996 adjustments to income. These include alimony paid and deductible IRA contributions　**4** $ _____

5　**Add** lines 3 and 4 and enter the total　**5** $ _____

6　Enter an estimate of your 1996 nonwage income (such as dividends or interest)　**6** $ _____

7　**Subtract** line 6 from line 5. Enter the result, but not less than -0-　**7** $ _____

8　**Divide** the amount on line 7 by $2,500 and enter the result here. Drop any fraction　**8** _____

9　Enter the number from Personal Allowances Worksheet, line G, on page 1　**9** _____

10　**Add** lines 8 and 9 and enter the total here. If you plan to use the Two-Earner/Two-Job Worksheet, also enter this total on line 1 below. Otherwise, **stop here** and enter this total on Form W-4, line 5, on page 1　**10** _____

Two-Earner/Two-Job Worksheet

Note: *Use this worksheet only if the instructions for line G on page 1 direct you here.*

1　Enter the number from line G on page 1 (or from line 10 above if you used the Deductions and Adjustments Worksheet)　**1** _____

2　Find the number in **Table 1** below that applies to the **LOWEST** paying job and enter it here　**2** _____

3　If line 1 is **GREATER THAN OR EQUAL TO** line 2, subtract line 2 from line 1. Enter the result here (if zero, enter -0-) and on Form W-4, line 5, on page 1. **DO NOT** use the rest of this worksheet　**3** _____

Note: *If line 1 is **LESS THAN** line 2, enter -0- on Form W-4, line 5, on page 1. Complete lines 4–9 to calculate the additional withholding amount necessary to avoid a year end tax bill.*

4　Enter the number from line 2 of this worksheet　**4** _____

5　Enter the number from line 1 of this worksheet　**5** _____

6　**Subtract** line 5 from line 4　**6** _____

7　Find the amount in **Table 2** below that applies to the **HIGHEST** paying job and enter it here　**7** $ _____

8　**Multiply** line 7 by line 6 and enter the result here. This is the additional annual withholding amount needed　**8** $ _____

9　Divide line 8 by the number of pay periods remaining in 1996. (For example, divide by 26 if you are paid every other week and you complete this form in December 1995.) Enter the result here and on Form W-4, line 6, page 1. This is the additional amount to be withheld from each paycheck　**9** $ _____

Table 1: Two-Earner/Two-Job Worksheet

Married Filing Jointly				All Others	
If wages from **LOWEST** paying job are—	Enter on line 2 above	If wages from **LOWEST** paying job are—	Enter on line 2 above	If wages from **LOWEST** paying job are—	Enter on line 2 above
0 - $3,000	0	30,001 - 50,000	9	0 - $4,000	0
3,001 - 6,000	1	50,001 - 55,000	10	4,001 - 10,000	1
6,001 - 11,000	2	55,001 - 60,000	11	10,001 - 14,000	2
11,001 - 16,000	3	60,001 - 70,000	12	14,001 - 19,000	3
16,001 - 21,000	4	70,001 - 80,000	13	19,001 - 23,000	4
21,001 - 27,000	5	80,001 - 90,000	14	23,001 - 45,000	5
27,001 - 31,000	6	90,001 and over	15	45,001 - 60,000	6
31,001 - 34,000	7			60,001 - 70,000	7
34,001 - 39,000	8			70,001 and over	8

Table 2: Two-Earner/Two-Job Worksheet

Married Filing Jointly		All Others	
If wages from **HIGHEST** paying job are—	Enter on line 7 above	If wages from **HIGHEST** paying job are—	Enter on line 7 above
0 - $50,000	$380	0 - $30,000	$380
50,001 - 100,000	710	30,001 - 60,000	710
100,001 - 130,000	790	60,001 - 120,000	790
130,001 - 240,000	920	120,001 - 240,000	920
240,001 and over	1,010	240,001 and over	1,010

Fringe Benefits

Employers can attract workers with employee benefits. Some surveys show that benefits are a major reason people work. This section explains the common benefits offered by employers.

Fringe benefits usually are available only to full-time employees. Some employers offer no fringe benefits at all. Your employer may make full payment for some of your fringe benefits; however, most employers now require employees to make partial contributions to help pay for them. Some employers offer cafeteria plans, giving you the choice of which benefits you want (see box). Below are the benefits most commonly offered:

- **Health insurance** pays doctor and hospital expenses. Most health insurance has a standard deductible. The deductible is the amount of medical expense you must pay before the insurance company will pay your medical bills. Some health plans cover the cost of prescription drugs and dental work. A variation of health insurance is the Health Maintenance Organization (HMO). HMOs typically cover all medical expenses—sometimes with a small copayment from you. An HMO plan is based on the assumption that seeking treatment as soon as symptoms appear prevents major problems later.

- **Disability insurance** pays part or all of your salary if you are sick or injured for several weeks or more. These payments usually begin after you have used all of your paid sick leave.

- **Life insurance** is particularly important if you have dependents, because you can designate a person (the beneficiary) to receive a payment from the insurance company should you die. Some employers pay for a life insurance policy equal to one year's salary.

- **Dependent care** comes in several forms. Some companies run childcare centers that provide low-cost care for their employees' children. As the workforce ages, many employees need care for elderly parents. Not many businesses have started adult daycare centers yet, but they are looking at the potential need. Organizations that don't run daycare facilities may reimburse employees for a portion of their childcare costs.

Here are two rules of thumb for choosing which fringe benefits to accept:

1. If the employer provides the benefit free of charge, you should sign up for it.

2. If the employer requires you to pay part or all of the benefit costs, only sign up for those you really need.

Paid Time Off

Your employer may offer paid time off for one or several of the following circumstances. This benefit varies greatly from one employer to another.

Key Definition

Cafeteria Plans

This is an increasingly popular benefit plan in which an employer provides a wide variety of choices and a set amount of money, and allows each employee to choose which benefits to "buy." *The Wall Street Journal* predicts these plans will continue to become more individualized.[4] Benefits will be adjusted as workers move through life stages. For example, a young worker starting a family can receive hospital coverage for pregnancy. Later in life, the same worker may want to put that money into a retirement plan.

■ **Holiday pay.** The organization designates holidays on which you are not required to work. Many organizations pay their employees for holiday time.

■ **Paid sick leave.** Employers normally establish a limited number of paid days that you may use for sick days each month or year. If you exceed the limit, you won't be paid for days you can't work due to illness. There are many different methods of accumulating sick time. Make sure you understand the one your employer uses.

■ **Vacation leave.** This is time off paid for by your employer. As a rule, the amount of vacation time increases with the number of years you work for an organization.

■ **Jury duty leave.** Some states require employers to pay employees for time served on a jury. Some employers do so voluntarily because they feel it is a community responsibility.

■ **Funeral leave.** This leave is given when a member of your immediate family dies. Various organizations define "immediate family" differently. Ask about your employer's policy.

■ **Military leave.** Members of the Reserve or National Guard are required to attend active duty training for at least two weeks each year. In a national crisis, that period can be extended by Congress. Some employers, though not required, pay for the time you are on active military leave or pay the difference in salary.

■ **Maternity, paternity, and adoption leave.** This is time off for your child's birth or adoption. The Family and Medical Leave Act requires that a company with more than 50 employees provide maternity, paternity, and adoption leave. A company does not have to pay for the leave. Smaller companies must treat maternity leave like sick leave.

Required Benefits

Some employee benefits are required by federal and state laws. Those required by federal law are discussed below.

■ **Federal Insurance Contributions Act (FICA).** The employer must match your contribution to the Social Security fund. This fund pays benefits to your children who are under age 21 should you die. The fund pays you and your dependents if you are disabled for more than 12 months. It also pays you a pension when you reach retirement age.

■ **Unemployment insurance.** Your employer must contribute to an unemployment insurance fund administered by your state or agree to pay your unemployment claims. If you are laid off or dismissed from your job, you may file a claim with your state employment agency. Eligibility requirements vary from state to state. The reasons for unemployment also are taken into consideration. Eligibility is determined by the state employment office. Unemployment benefit amounts are established by each state. Weekly benefits are paid for 26 weeks or until you find suitable employment, whichever comes first.

■ **Worker's compensation insurance.** Most states require employers to carry this insurance, which pays for injuries that occur on the job. In addition, you receive partial payment for time off the job caused by work-related injuries.

Voluntary Deductions

In addition to fringe benefit deductions, your employer can deduct other withholdings from your paycheck with your approval. Some deductions, such as federal and state taxes, are required. Others, like those listed next, are voluntary.

■ **Child support.** You may want to have monthly child support payments automatically deducted from your paycheck. Check with your lawyer or court representative to find out how this is done.

■ **Savings plan.** You may have a portion of your pay sent directly to your bank or credit union account. Use it to make automatic loan payments, add to savings, or for some other use.

■ **Charity donations.** You can make deductions to contribute to a charity. This arrangement is most often available for United Way organizations.

■ **Union dues.** Most unions make arrangements with employers to withhold dues directly from your paycheck. In some areas, unions have agreements with employers requiring them to withhold dues *even if you are not a union member.*

■ **Retirement fund.** Sometimes an employer contributes a percentage of your wage or salary to a retirement fund. Usually you must contribute to the fund, and then the employer contributes an amount equal to what you contribute. There usually is a limit to the amount the employer contributes. Typically, you must work for the employer a minimum number of years to become "vested." This means that if you leave before the minimum number of years, you can take your contribution to the fund, but not the employer's.

■ **Stock options.** You may be able to have deductions withheld to purchase company stock. Your employer may require you to be employed by the organization for several years before you are eligible for this benefit.

Employee Services

Employers provide many different services for their employees. Many employers feel that the more they do for their employees, the more the employees do for them. Below is just a partial listing of services your employer may provide.

■ **Educational assistance plans.** Employers often reimburse college or technical school tuition for those employees who are working toward a degree or taking work-related courses. They also may reimburse employees for textbooks.

■ **Employee assistance programs.** Employees may receive counseling for personal or work-related problems, including treatment for drug abuse or alcoholism.

■ **Credit unions.** Credit unions provide financial services for employees, usually at a lower cost than banks or savings and loan institutions. Frequently interest on savings accounts is higher and interest on loans is lower.

■ **Others.** These may include legal assistance, health services, a food service, financial planning, housing and moving expenses, transportation, purchase discounts, and recreational services.

The following table shows the percentage of employers who offer fringe benefits. [5]

Benefit	Small Businesses	Large Businesses
Paid vacations	88%	92%
Paid holidays	82	96
Paid sick leave	53	67
Medical care	71	83
Dental care	33	60
Life insurance	64	94
Retirement plan	45	59

Selecting Benefits and Deductions

In the list below, place a check mark beside the fringe benefits or deductions you want, even if you must pay a portion of the cost. Write your reasons for selecting or not selecting each item.

❑ Health insurance

_____

_____

❑ Dental insurance

_____

_____

❏ Prescription drugs

_____

_____

❏ Life insurance

_____

_____

❏ Disability insurance

_____

_____

❏ Retirement program

_____

_____

❏ Childcare

_____

_____

❏ Union dues

_____

_____

❏ Savings plan

_____

_____

❏ Charity donation

_____

_____

❏ Stock options

_____

_____

Now check the paid time off and employee assistance benefits your employer provides. If you aren't currently employed, check those you think are important for an employer to provide.

❏ Holiday leave

_____

_____

❏ Vacation leave

_____

_____

❏ Jury duty leave

_____

_____

❏ Sick leave

_____

_____

❏ Funeral leave

_____

_____

❏ Military leave

_____

_____

❏ Family leave

_____

_____

❏ Medical leave (long-term)

_____

_____

❑ Educational assistance

_____

_____

❑ Employee assistance plan

_____

_____

❑ Credit unions

_____

_____

❑ Others (specify)

_____

_____

Applying What You've Learned

Steve and his wife have a 7-year-old daughter and 3-year-old son. Steve is a carpenter for a construction firm and is working on a construction technology degree at a local community college. During the past year, the children have been sick several times. Steve and his wife just purchased a new home.

1. List six employee benefits or services that Steve needs.

   _____   _____

   _____   _____

   _____   _____

2. Tell why each benefit is important to Steve.

   _____

   _____

   _____

   _____

Pilar is the branch manager of a bank. She is divorced and has a 4-year-old daughter. Pilar is active in the Naval Reserve. During the past year she has been mildly depressed about her divorce and has been drinking more than she would like.

1. What benefits would be the most helpful for Pilar?

    _____   _____

    _____   _____

    _____   _____

2. Explain why these benefits are important.

    _____

    _____

    _____

    _____

    _____

Introduction to the Job

After orientation, your supervisor is likely to take you on a tour of the job site or work area. He or she should provide you with the following information, but be prepared to ask about these things anyway.

Work Instructions

It's important that you understand how to do your job. Your supervisor should show and tell you how to do the tasks that make up the job. Here are a few guidelines to follow during this time.

■ **Don't panic.** You won't be expected to learn everything at once. And you aren't expected to do everything right the first time.

■ **Listen carefully and watch closely** as the supervisor demonstrates a task.

■ **Ask questions** when you don't understand something you've been told or shown.

■ **Learn what is expected.** Make sure you know exactly what the supervisor expects from you.

Supplies and Equipment

You need to know how and where to get the supplies and equipment you need to do your job. Some things you might need to know are listed below:

■ Where supplies are kept

■ Procedures for checking out supplies and equipment

■ Who is in charge of supply distribution

The Phone System

All businesses rely on communication. Even if your job doesn't involve the telephone, you'll need to know the following information:

■ **How to use the phone system.** You already know how to use a phone, I'm sure. But office phone systems can be incredibly complex and intimidating, with rows of buttons and lights, dozens of features, and as much wiring as a small computer. Ask a coworker to show you how to use the most common features of the phone system.

■ **Telephone policy.** Who answers your phone if you're away from your desk? What should you say when you answer the phone? Can you make and receive personal calls? Is there an access code you must enter when making long-distance calls?

Breaks

Different companies have different policies for taking breaks. In one, you might be able to take your breaks whenever you want to, as long as you're responsible about it. In another, you might have to take your breaks only at specified times. In a factory, an entire line might take breaks together. Many organizations prohibit smoking on the job or restrict it to a smoking room. If you intend to smoke during your break, you need to know where it's allowed.

■ **Rest room break.** In some jobs you must find a replacement to do your job before taking such a break.

■ **Rest break.** Employers often provide two 15-minute breaks (in addition to a meal break) in an eight-hour shift. Find out when you can take a break and if there is a break room.

■ **Meal break.** You will probably be allowed a meal break around the middle of your workday if you work an eight-hour shift. Ask when you can take a meal break and how much time is allowed.

Some organizations have in-house cafeterias. Others provide break rooms where you can eat lunch. Find out if your employer provides a kitchen with a refrigerator or microwave oven for employee use.

Your supervisor should explain what you need to know about work tasks, supplies, telephone systems, and breaks. If he or she forgets, don't be afraid to ask. This is an important rule during the first few days on the job.

Off to a Good Start

After your supervisor shows you around, you'll be on your own, and you'll start your new job the same way everyone else does. You won't know much about the job. You probably won't know anyone there. You may wonder if you can do the job and if you'll like it. Here are some suggestions to help you adjust during the first few weeks.

■ **Be positive.** Expect good things to happen. Starting a new job gives you an opportunity to prove yourself to your supervisor and coworkers.

■ **Ask for help.** Your supervisor and coworkers expect you to ask questions. They expect and are willing to help when you ask. Listen carefully, so you don't have to ask the same question more than once.

■ **Don't be a know-it-all.** You are new on the job. No matter how much you know and how skilled you are, you don't know everything about this particular job. Take the first few weeks to learn. Gain the respect of your coworkers and supervisor by demonstrating your ability to do your job well. Then you can begin making suggestions to improve the way things are done.

Have a sense of humor. New workers may be tested by other workers. Some want to see how you respond to teasing and practical jokes. You might consider this an initiation. Try your best to accept good-natured teasing. If things get out of hand and you feel unfairly treated or abused, talk with your supervisor about the situation.

Find a friend. Look for someone who seems to know the job well and ask him or her to help you if you need it. Sometimes your supervisor will assign someone to help you the first few days.

Follow instructions. Your supervisor is the most important person in your work life. He or she decides whether you stay on the job, get promoted, and receive raises. Follow instructions, be helpful, and do your best possible job.

Read company policies. If your company has a booklet explaining policies and procedures, read through it carefully. Ignorance is not an excuse for doing something wrong or not knowing what to do.

Determine evaluation policies. Find out what is expected of you in the first few days, weeks, and months. What standards are used to measure your success, and who does the evaluation?[6]

The first few days on the job are important. They often determine the way you feel about the job. Staying positive, asking questions, and listening helps ensure your first few days on the job are a positive experience.

Applying What You've Learned

On Craig's first day as a stock clerk, his supervisor, Sharon, introduced him to the other workers, then walked him around the store and explained how the shelves should be stocked, when to stock the products, where to get new items, and how to price the items. Sharon then left Craig on his own. Everything went fine until he came to a brand he wasn't sure how to price. Craig didn't want to appear stupid, so he went ahead and marked the prices the same as another brand.

1. What would you have done if you were Craig?

_____

_____

_____

2. What problems do you think Craig might have caused?

_____

_____

_____

Vicky is a new secretary for a law firm. Her supervisor gave her a tour of the office, introduced her to other workers, and told her what tasks she would be doing. She then told Vicky to contact her if she had questions. List five questions Vicky should ask her supervisor.

1. _____

2. _____

3. _____

4. _____

5. _____

Summing Up

Preparation is the key to creating a positive first impression on a new job. Of course you can't prepare for every situation, but the more issues you're aware of and the more questions you ask before you start work, the better you'll do on the job.

Notes

1. "1996 Industry Report," *Training* (October 1996), 41.

2. Robert L. Mathis and John H. Jackson, *Personnel: Human Resource Management* (St. Paul, MN: West Publishing, 1983).

3. Robert L. Mathis and Nick Nykodym, "Put Drug Detection to the Test," *Personnel Journal* (August 1987), 91-97.

4. "More Benefits Bend with Workers' Needs," *The Wall Street Journal* (January 9, 1990), B1.

5. William J. Miatrowski, "Small Businesses and Their Employees," *Monthly Labor Review* (October 1994), 29-35.

6. Carole Y. Lyles, "The First Days on the Job," *US Black Engineer* (June 30, 1992), PG.

Chapter 4

Making a Good Impression

Our impressions affect the way we treat people. This is a natural human reaction. So it should come as no surprise that the impressions other people have about you affect the way they treat you. People form impressions based on looks and actions. Your physical appearance often determines what kind of first impression you make. It's important that you look as good as possible to make a positive impression.

Hygiene (personal body care) also influences your impression on people. Messy hair, bad breath, and body odor make a poor impression. In this chapter, we'll look at dressing for success and at the basics of good hygiene. Dress and hygiene may seem basic, but it's often the basics that are important for success at work.[1]

Premeaux and Mondy put it this way: "In certain situations, dress can even be as important to job success as worker skills. Superiors and subordinates make certain decisions based solely on appearance. So it is to the worker's advantage to dress appropriately."[2] In other words, people assume you care for your job in the same way you care for yourself.

I Haven't a Thing to Wear

Dress for work has changed dramatically in the last decade, becoming decidedly more casual. The following survey of human resource managers demonstrates this.[3]

Casual Dress Days	1995	1992
Casual everyday	33%	20%
One day per week	42	17
No casual days	10	37
Occasional	15	27

But even if dress is more casual, it's important to remember that clothes influence the way people perceive you. These perceptions affect how well you are accepted by your supervisor and coworkers. Below are some general guidelines about what to wear on the job.

- **Dress codes.** The best way to know how to dress is to ask. Your supervisor and coworkers know about official and unofficial dress codes for your job. For example, many "casual" dress codes still don't allow workers to wear jeans or shorts to the office. Unofficial dress codes can affect work assignments, pay raises, and promotions.

- **Appropriate dress.** You probably have some very nice clothes that are not appropriate for the workplace. Clothes you would wear for a night on the town probably aren't appropriate for the workplace. Neither are tight-fitting clothes, low-cut dresses, unbuttoned shirts, short skirts, and neon-hued outfits.

■ **Neat dress.** Make sure the clothes you wear are neat and clean. Press them if necessary. Even casual dress must be appropriate. Your clothes should be in good shape, with no tears or stains. Your shoes should be clean and in good condition, and polished if they are leather.

■ **Uniforms.** Some businesses require employees to wear uniforms at work. Here are some things you need to know about uniforms.

—Who is responsible for keeping uniforms clean and pressed? Some employers have a cleaning service, others expect you to keep your uniform in good shape.

—How many uniforms do you need?

—Who is responsible for accidental damage to the uniform?

—How should the uniform be worn? (Do you need special shoes or blouses with it?)

■ **Safety clothing.** Some jobs present possible safety hazards, and you may be required to wear certain clothing. Here are some common safety considerations.

—Loose clothing or dangling jewelry may get caught and pull you into moving equipment. Avoid wearing such items if you work around moving equipment.

—Hard leather shoes are a must on the job if something heavy could drop on your feet. You may be required to wear steel-toed shoes for protection.

—Jeans help protect you from scratches and cuts that may occur on some jobs.

Special Safety Equipment

Certain jobs require protective dress considerations. Find out what safety equipment is required on the job, *then wear it*. Safety equipment may be slightly uncomfortable, but failure to wear the equipment can result in losing your job. Your employer is responsible for your safety and will not tolerate safety infractions. Following is a list of common safety equipment:

■ **Safety glasses** are required for jobs in which small particles could strike or lodge in your eyes. For example, workers drilling on metal parts wear safety glasses.

■ **Ear protectors** are needed if your job exposes you to continuous or loud noise, which can cause hearing problems. Ground personnel who work around jet airplanes wear ear protectors.

■ **Hard hats** are necessary if you work where falling objects are a risk. A hard hat may not protect you from all injuries, but it can reduce the seriousness of an injury. Most construction workers are required to wear hard hats.

■ **Masks** are a must if you work where exposure to fumes from dangerous chemicals is unavoidable. Failure to wear a mask in some jobs could result in serious injury or even death. A painter in a body and trim shop typically wears a mask.

■ **Gloves** protect against the frostbite, blisters, or rope burns that are hazards of some jobs. A person stacking hay bales or working in the frozen food section of a grocery store probably wears gloves.

■ **Protective clothing** is worn by those who work with or near hazardous materials. This clothing includes gloves, aprons, coveralls, boots, or an entire protective suit. If you work with hazardous materials, your employer must provide the protective clothing you need and teach you how to protect yourself from harm.

Applying What You've Learned

Jill is an accountant at a life insurance company. Check the items you think she should wear to work.

_____ Blouse	_____ Shirt
_____ Boots	_____ Shorts
_____ Business suit	_____ Skirt
_____ Casual shoes	_____ Slacks
_____ Dress	_____ Socks
_____ Dress shirt	_____ Sweater
_____ Jacket	_____ T-shirt
_____ Jeans	_____ Tie

_____ Jewelry   _____ Vest

_____ Leather shoes   _____ Tennis shoes

_____ Nylons   _____ Sandals

_____ Pants   _____ Other

Why did you select these items? _____

_____

_____

_____

Tyler is a counter attendant in a dry-cleaning shop. Check the items you think he should wear to work.

_____ Blouse   _____ Shirt

_____ Boots   _____ Shorts

_____ Business suit   _____ Skirt

_____ Casual shoes   _____ Slacks

_____ Dress   _____ Socks

_____ Dress shirt   _____ Sweater

_____ Jacket   _____ T-shirt

_____ Jeans   _____ Tie

_____ Jewelry   _____ Vest

_____ Leather shoes   _____ Tennis shoes

_____ Nylons   _____ Sandals

_____ Pants   _____ Other _____

Why did you select these items? _____

_____

_____

_____

Cal is a production worker in an automotive parts factory. Check the items you think he should wear to work.

_____ Blouse   _____ Shirt

_____ Boots   _____ Shorts

_____ Business suit   _____ Skirt

61

_____ Casual shoes   _____ Slacks

_____ Dress   _____ Socks

_____ Dress shirt   _____ Sweater

_____ Jacket   _____ T-shirt

_____ Jeans   _____ Tie

_____ Jewelry   _____ Vest

_____ Leather shoes   _____ Tennis shoes

_____ Nylons   _____ Sandals

_____ Pants   _____ Other _____

Why did you select these items?

_____

_____

_____

Brandtrell is a lab assistant at a hospital. Check the items you think he should wear to work.

_____ Blouse   _____ Shirt

_____ Boots   _____ Shorts

_____ Business suit   _____ Skirt

_____ Casual shoes   _____ Slacks

_____ Dress   _____ Socks

_____ Dress shirt   _____ Sweater

_____ Jacket   _____ T-shirt

_____ Jeans   _____ Tie

_____ Jewelry   _____ Vest

_____ Leather shoes   _____ Tennis shoes

_____ Nylons   _____ Sandals

_____ Pants   _____ Other _____

Why did you select these items? _____

_____

_____

_____

Personal Grooming

Grooming habits that your friends accept or that seemed adequate while you were in school may cause problems at work. Imagine a typical morning as you prepare for work or school.

1. List the hygiene and grooming activities you practice.

   _____

   _____

   _____

2. What other kinds of grooming do you practice on a periodic basis? How often?

   _____

   _____

3. How would you rate your appearance after going through the activities listed above? Check the item that best describes yourself.

   ____ **I look perfect.** Anyone would like to be with me.

   ____ **I look good.** My friends, coworkers, and supervisor would like to be with me.

   ____ **I look fine.** At least my friends and family would like to be with me.

   ____ **I could look better.** I like to be with myself, anyway.

   ____ **I don't look very good.** Even my dog wouldn't like to be with me.

4. How can you improve your grooming so your appearance would be acceptable to anyone?

   _____

   _____

   _____

63

Below is a checklist of grooming activities you should practice on a regular basis. Place a plus (+) next to those you do regularly and a minus (-) next to those you could improve.

____ **Shower or bathe regularly**. It's not pleasant to work with someone who has body odor.

____ **Use deodorant daily.** This helps control body odor that results from sweating.

____ **Brush your teeth** at least once a day and when possible after each meal. Bad breath won't win you any points at work.

____ **Gargle with mouthwash.** If you have a problem with bad breath, use mouthwash once or twice a day.

____ **Shave.** Facial hair can be a distraction in the work setting. A recent court decision determined that a policy against facial hair may be unconstitutional. However, at many jobs you're expected to remain clean-shaven. This means shaving regularly, typically whenever stubble appears. A mustache is acceptable in most jobs, a beard may not be. And food preparation or serving jobs may require you to wear a hair net over your beard. If you want to wear a beard or mustache, remember to groom them on a daily basis and keep them neatly trimmed.

____ **Wash your hair** every one to three days. The oiliness of your hair determines how often you need to shampoo.

____ **Style your hair neatly.** Your hair will always look better if you keep it trimmed and take time to style it. Talk with a hair stylist about keeping your hair looking good every day. At the least, comb your hair several times a day. Wear hair styles appropriate for the workplace and your lifestyle.

____ **Trim your hair** on a regular basis. Extremely long hair on either sex may be considered unconventional in some organizations. Long hair worn loose may be a safety problem in certain jobs. It's also a hygienic problem in jobs such as food preparation and serving, for which you may have to wear a hair net.

____ **Trim and clean your fingernails.** Women who wear fingernail polish should use conservative colors for work.

____ **Use makeup sparingly.**
Makeup can help you look your best, but not when it's applied wrong. Natural colors that compliment your skin tone are appropriate. Bold colors, such as hot pinks and bright blues, are rarely appropriate in the workplace. If you're not sure how to apply makeup to enhance your looks, ask the consultant at a cosmetic counter.

____ **Pierce sparingly.** Pierced earrings for women are almost the norm these days; and even for men, they have become more acceptable. However, if you are a man with a pierced ear, it might be a good idea to remove your earring for interviews and for the first few days on the job, since many people are still uncomfortable with pierced ears for men. Women should not wear long, dangly, flashy earrings to work.

Other types of piercing—for example lips, eyebrows, and nose—are less acceptable. Body piercing may hinder you in some workplaces, but it's considered reasonable in others. Use your own best judgment for your workplace. Exceptions may be made if piercing represents an employee's cultural or religious beliefs.[4]

Special Hygiene Concerns

In some jobs your own health, as well as that of customers or patients, depends upon your good hygienic practices. For example, health care organizations and food preparation facilities are required by law to enforce certain sanitary practices. Below is a list of the most commonly required hygienic practices.

A Word About Cologne: Moderation

Colognes and perfumes can be pleasant, but too much of either is offensive to many people.[5] Overpowering odor is not appropriate in the workplace, no matter what the source. Some people have allergies to colognes and perfumes. You should be considerate of coworkers and not aggravate this condition. This is such a problem for some people that they are lobbying for laws to protect them against unwelcome odors.

- **Hair nets** are sometimes required for jobs in food service or preparation.

- **Washing hands.** You must wash your hands with soap and water after using the rest room. This helps protect you from disease or from spreading germs and is particularly important in jobs where you prepare or serve food. Use soap and lather your hands for 10 to 15 seconds. Regulations require workers in health occupations to wash their hands each time they work with a patient.

■ **Gloves** help control exposure to germs in food preparation and health occupations.

■ **Aprons** may be required in food preparation jobs to prevent germs, dirt, or other foreign particles on your clothes from getting into the food.

Additional precautions are taken in many occupations. You should become familiar with the hygiene practices required for your job. In some cases (such as food preparation jobs) there will be state and local laws that govern hygiene.

Special Personal Considerations

There are three specific issues regarding appearance that justify special attention here: physical condition, weight, and acne. Let's examine these one at a time.

1. **Physical condition.** This applies to everyone. You should exercise regularly to be in good physical condition. Exercise improves your stamina and allows you to work harder and longer. This pays off when you are rewarded with higher pay or promotions because of your productivity. Being in good shape applies to workers in both physically and mentally demanding jobs.

2. **Weight.** People who are overweight often encounter negative reactions from other people. Yes, it's discriminatory, but many in our society think overweight people are less attractive. Some even perceive overweight people as lazy. This is quite an obstacle for the hopeful employee to overcome. If you are overweight, you should do as much as possible to improve your appearance. This may mean going on a diet and exercising more. (Consult your physician before starting any weight-reduction program.) It also means wearing clothes that fit well and look good on you. Do your best to overcome any weight problem.

3. **Acne.** Many people have a problem with acne. If you have a serious acne problem, consult a dermatologist. A better diet and skin care and medication may help improve this condition.

While physical attractiveness may be a factor in getting ahead at work, a positive self-image and good mental attitude are more important. If you have a problem with your appearance, do your best to look as good as you can. Then concentrate on other things. No one can do more than their best.

Mannerisms and Habits

Mannerisms and habits can have as powerful an influence on people as appearance. Look at other people and determine what mannerisms they exhibit that negatively affect the way you feel about them. Examine yourself for any such behavior. Ask friends and family to tell you if they observe undesirable traits in your conduct. (Family members will be especially willing to do this.) Listed below are some common problems.

■ **Using tobacco products**. Many organizations have banned smoking on the job. In some cases, smoking is restricted to certain areas outside of buildings. People often are looked down on because of smoking.[6] Chewing tobacco or using snuff also may be prohibited and creates a negative image.

■ **Wearing earphones.** Many people use portable radios and cassette and CD players on the job.[7] Be aware that this can reduce communication and create safety hazards. Your employer may also interpret it to mean you are disinterested in your job.

■ **Chewing gum.** It's hard to speak clearly when you've got a wad of gum in your mouth. You also run the risk of looking like a cow chewing cud. Be smart: Leave the gum at home.

■ **Using slang or profanity.** Many people will think of you as ignorant or uneducated if you use slang. You should use a commonly understood vocabulary. A person who uses profanity is even worse, appearing not only ignorant but also rude and uncouth.

■ **Picking and pulling.** Sometimes people unconsciously develop a habit of picking at a certain part of their body, maybe their ears, nose, hair, chin, or fingers. This can be a real turn-off to other people.

Applying What You've Learned

Sasha started work as a secretary in a large office about four weeks ago. Today she came into work wearing a short skirt that is quite revealing when she sits down. She has on so much perfume you can smell it 20 feet away. Her nails are very long and painted purple, to match her eye shadow and her dress. Her lipstick is also purple. She is wearing spiked heels and black mesh stockings.

1. What is your first reaction when you see Sasha? _____
   _____
   _____

2. Your supervisor just told you that Sasha will be helping you complete a proposal for a potential client. Do you think Sasha will be a good worker? Explain the reason for your answer. _____
   _____
   _____

Dan is a maintenance worker at a hospital. He is required to wear a uniform to work. His hair is shaggy and unkempt. Some employees avoid him, saying that he smells bad. Once in a while he comes to work with a three-day growth of stubble on his face.

1. List what Dan should do to properly groom himself for this job. _____
   _____
   _____

2. Are there any on-the-job hygienic issues Dan should keep in mind? _____
   _____
   _____

Summing Up

Proper dress and good hygiene are crucial for two important reasons. First, they affect your appearance, and your appearance has an effect on supervisors, coworkers, and customers—either good or bad. Second, proper dress and hygiene may be important to your health and safety. Wearing clothes that can protect you from injury or disease is important. Find out what the safety and health requirements are for your job and follow them closely. Remember, how you dress, how you take care of yourself, and how you use mannerisms tell others a lot about you: Make sure what you're conveying about yourself is positive.

Notes

1. Rhonda Reynolds, "The Looks That Kill Careers," *Black Enterprise* (June 1995), 281-288

2. Shane R. Premeaux and R. Wayne Mondy, "People Problems: Dress Distractions," *Management Solutions* (January 1987), 35-37.

3. Kevin Johnson, "Dressing Down in the Office," *USA Today* (February 23, 1996), 1B.

4. "Business Bulletin," *The Wall Street Journal* (July 18, 1996), A1.

5. Leah Rosch, "The Professional Image Report," *Working Woman* (October 1988), 109.

6. "Smoked Out," *The Economist* (March 26, 1994), 29-30.

7. Cheryl Powell, "When Workers Wear Walkmans on the Job," *The Wall Street Journal* (July 11, 1994), B1.

Chapter 5

Being There ...
On Time!

An organization can't operate without dependable workers. A supervisor must be able to rely on employees coming to work every day on time. When a worker is late or absent, it causes many problems. In fact, employers list absenteeism as one of the major reasons for firing employees.

Consider the following scenario:

George supervises the morning shift in a fast food restaurant. The phone rings at 6 A.M. "George, this is Lee. My car won't start so I won't be at work today." The breakfast crowd has started to arrive in the dining room. Several cars are lined up at the drive through window.

1. What problems did Lee create by not coming to work? _____

_____

_____

_____

2. How does Lee's absence affect his coworkers? _____

_____

_____

_____

3. How many times do you think George will allow Lee to be absent from work before taking some kind of action? _____

_____

_____

_____

There are several problems you could have listed that Lee's absence caused. Your list might have included these:

■ **Problems for the employer.** Employee absence can cost an organization money in two ways:

1. **Reduced productivity.** Fewer workers means the organization produces fewer goods or cannot serve as many customers. In some instances the amount of goods and services remains the same but the quality suffers.

2. **Customer dissatisfaction.** Customers won't be served as well as they should be. For instance, if a worker in a production job is absent, a customer's shipment may not be made on time because there isn't enough help.

- **Problems for supervisors.** Worker absence means supervisors must rearrange work schedules and plans. Another worker may have to fill in. Problems created by one absence usually continue throughout the day. Supervisors pick up the slack, which may make them angry. How the supervisor reacts depends largely on the reason and frequency of the absence.

- **Problems for coworkers.** Everyone must work harder when another worker is absent. A person who had the day off may be called into work. Someone who just finished a shift may be asked to stay and work a double shift. They, too, may be angry at the absent employee.

- **Problems for the employee.** Being absent or late often results in "docked" pay. This means no pay for the time off work. The organization's policy about days off will affect how much the paycheck is reduced. Repeated incidents could result in the absent worker's termination.

Customer Satisfaction

Americans know the importance of satisfying customers. Tom Peters, a leading management expert, emphasized the need for good customer service to be competitive in today's business world.[1] Think about it. Do you go to stores where clerks treat you poorly? Do you return to a restaurant that takes a long time to bring your food? Of course not. That's why it's important for businesses to provide good customer service. They want customers to come back. Good customer service is difficult for a business to provide without dependable workers.

What's Your Excuse?

Sometimes being absent or late is unavoidable; more often, it's not. Read the following list of excuses. Place a check mark in the *Absent* column if that reason causes you to be absent frequently. Check *Late* if it makes you late, and *Both* if it causes you to be both late and absent on different occasions. If you aren't currently employed, check those reasons you were late or absent from a former job or from school.

Excuse	Absent	Late	Both
Overslept			
Missed the bus			
Personal illness			
Alarm didn't ring			
Children were sick			
Car wouldn't start			
Couldn't find a baby-sitter			
Someone borrowed my car			
Wanted to sleep in			
Traffic was bad			
Didn't feel like going			
Family problems			
Wanted to do other things			
Weather was bad			
Forgot the work schedule			
No clean clothes			
Had a hangover			
Took a trip instead			
Needed a day off			

As you look over this list, be aware of what you need to do to reduce the number of days you are absent from or late for work. You may find it interesting to compare your answers with the following reasons workers gave for their absenteeism.[2]

Reason for Absenteeism	Percentage of Days Absent
Illness	45%
Dealing with family issues	27
Taking care of personal business	13
Escaping stress	6
Various other reasons	9

On the average, employees miss 2.8 hours for every 100 hours worked. These absences cost employers almost $700 a year per employee. The next section reviews ways you can avoid the problems listed in the previous exercise.

Your Lifestyle Affects Your Work

A lifestyle is made up of the habits and activities you develop for day-to-day living, and includes what you eat, when and how long you sleep, and how you spend your time. Doctors and scientists know that your lifestyle can affect the amount of stress in your daily life. Peter Hanson, physician and lecturer on stress, points out that stress affects your health *and* your emotions.[3] Many of the reasons people miss work are directly related to their lifestyles. Here are some ways you can shape your lifestyle to increase your success at work.

- **Get a good night's sleep.** Most people need 6 to 8 hours of sleep each night. Stanley Coren, a psychologist and sleep researcher, believes that some people may need as many as 9 to 10 hours of sleep each night.[4] He believes that not getting enough sleep reduces work effectiveness as much as going to work drunk. Your body rests better when you sleep on a regular schedule. Many young people make the mistake of partying on work nights, which means they get less sleep, then skip work the next morning or are late.

- **Eat well.** Eat well-balanced meals on a regular schedule and avoid too much junk food. Consume plenty of fruits and vegetables. You are less likely to be ill when you have good eating habits.

- **Exercise regularly.** Most jobs in the United States are service- and information-related and don't require much exercise. Regular exercise keeps you in top physical and mental condition and helps you release job-related stress.

- **Don't smoke.** *Reader's Digest* cites a Robert Half International survey that reports that one in four employers will reject a smoker who is competing for a job against an equally qualified nonsmoker.[5] There is plenty of medical evidence that smoking is hazardous to both smokers and nonsmokers. Many organizations offer incentives and help for employees who want to quit smoking.

■ **Don't drink too much.** Alcohol can cause health problems. The more alcohol you drink, the more you may damage your body. Drinking to excess will reduce your performance on the job the next day. Drinking during or before work is often cause for dismissal.

■ **Don't do drugs.** Illegal drugs are harmful to the body and mind. You should not take any drugs unless they are specifically prescribed for you by a physician. Policies on illegal drug use vary among organizations. If you test positive for certain drugs, some organizations will give you a choice of entering a rehabilitation program or being fired. Other employers will simply fire you outright.

■ **Keep good company.** Your relationships affect your work. For instance, if your friends don't work, they may want you to adapt to their schedule, which may leave you too tired for work the next day. If you're facing a conflict like this, you need to establish a priority for work and social activities. Avoid people who may get you into trouble with the law. Employers *do not* appreciate workers who miss work because they are in jail. In fact, you could get fired for missing work for that reason if your employer finds out.

■ **Socialize with coworkers.** We all need time to socialize with friends and acquaintances. Our coworkers often become our best friends because we spend so much time with them. Relationships with coworkers can be positive, or they can quickly turn sour. Here are guidelines to help you avoid problems in your work relationships.

— **Approach romances with coworkers cautiously.** They can make relationships with other coworkers awkward and often create unpleasant situations when the romance ends.

— **Don't limit your friendships to coworkers.** One thing that can happen when you socialize with coworkers is that you spend a lot of time talking about work. You need to get away from your job to reduce stress. This means not talking or even thinking about the job sometimes.

— **Don't let friendships with coworkers interfere with your work performance.** Don't do someone else's work to cover for their inability or laziness. Don't side with a friend in a feud with another worker or supervisor. Try to be neutral in work relationships.

Your Lifestyle and Stress

A moderate lifestyle will serve you well throughout your life. Rate your lifestyle using the following checklist. Check each statement that is true for you. Then score your answers to see how you measure up in terms of a healthy lifestyle.

_____ I do something fun on a regular basis.

_____ I rarely drink to excess.

_____ I exercise regularly.

_____ I have friends I can rely on.

_____ I gain strength from my religious beliefs.

_____ I avoid eating lots of junk food.

_____ I don't smoke.

_____ I average seven or more hours of sleep on work nights.

_____ I do not use illegal drugs.

_____ I eat at least one well-balanced meal daily.

Count the number of statements you checked. Score yourself using the following guidelines:

- **8 or more** reflects a positive lifestyle that will help you be effective on the job.

- **6 to 7** reflects a moderate lifestyle that will help you on the job.

- **5 or less** reflects a vulnerable lifestyle. You may find your lifestyle creates some job problems.

Plan for Success

Managing your life through good planning will help you avoid missing work. There are five major steps you can take to ensure a good work attendance record:

1. **Ensure reliable transportation.** It's not your employer's fault if your car won't start. *You are responsible for getting to work.* Transportation problems can occur even if you own a new car. Here are some steps you can take to ensure that you have reliable transportation.

   ■ **Keep your car in good operating condition.** Maintain it regularly. If you suspect you might have car trouble, try starting the car a couple of hours before work. This will give you time to find another method of transportation if you need to. Cold or wet days can mean problems starting a car, so check the car out early.

   ■ **Know your public transportation system.** Keep a schedule of the public transportation available to you. Highlight the times you would need to use the bus, train, or subway to get to work.

   ■ **Call a coworker for a ride.** Find a coworker who lives near you and has a reliable car. Make an agreement with them to share a ride if either of you has car trouble. You may want to carpool with other coworkers.

   ■ **Carpool.** Check with friends or advertise in the classifieds for someone who can share a ride to work with you. This arrangement will work even when you don't work together. You just need to work in the same general area.

   ■ **Walk or bicycle.** Think about finding housing near your workplace. Even if you live two to four miles from your job, you can still walk or ride a bike in good weather. If you don't want to move, find a job near your home. You may actually be able to work for less money at a job that doesn't cost you transportation expenses. Your net income (wages minus expenses connected with work) may be greater when you take a job close to home.

   ■ **If all else fails, call a cab.** A taxi is costly, but it usually won't cost as much as losing a day's pay. And it's certainly less costly than losing your job. You don't want to take a taxi to work every day, but you shouldn't hesitate to do so in an emergency.

2. **Make arrangements for reliable dependent care.** Most often, your dependents are your children. However, you may be caring for an elderly parent or a disabled spouse. If you are responsible for dependents, you need reliable care. What happens if a baby-sitter or home health aide lets you down? What if bad weather closes a daycare center? What if your dependent is ill? What if children can't get to school on the normal schedule? You should make plans ahead of time for substitute dependent care so you don't get caught off guard.

   - **Hire good aides.** Choose a reliable baby-sitter or home health aide. You can check reliability by asking for the person's references. These should be from people who have employed the person in their own homes.

   - **Select a good care center.** Ask for references. Learn about their policy for closing. What is their policy if your child, parent, or spouse is ill? There are now centers that will care for children when they are ill. You may pay more for centers with this service, but in the long run they may pay for themselves by reducing your absenteeism.

   - **Investigate health care programs.** In some cases, hospitals and specialized care centers will take care of your sick dependents while you are at work. Many of these programs you will use only when your child is sick. They cost more than normal childcare, but they are less costly than an unpaid day off work or losing your job.

   - **Have an emergency plan.** Find a friend or relative who is willing to care for your dependent for one or two days in case of emergency. The best plan is to have at least two people who are willing to do this.

3. **Use a calendar.** Have a calendar and use it to keep track of your work schedule. Record all assigned work days and any personal appointments that may conflict with work. Doctor and dental appointments can be noted in time to make arrangements with your employer. Whenever possible, schedule personal appointments outside of regular work hours.

   You may want to note other personal business on your calendar. A calendar is one of the best tools to help you plan your workday. Use the forms that follow to plan your weekly and monthly schedules.

79

Weekly Planner

Monday   Date _____
Time: *Appointments/Notes:*

_____   _____

_____   _____

_____   _____

_____   _____

_____   _____

_____   _____

Tuesday   Date _____
Time: *Appointments/Notes:*

_____   _____

_____   _____

_____   _____

_____   _____

_____   _____

_____   _____

Wednesday   Date _____
Time: *Appointments/Notes:*

_____   _____

_____   _____

_____   _____

_____   _____

_____   _____

Weekly Planner

Thursday

Time:

Date _____

Appointments/Notes

_____   _____

_____   _____

_____   _____

_____   _____

_____   _____

_____   _____

Friday

Time:

Date _____

Appointments/Notes:

_____   _____

_____   _____

_____   _____

_____   _____

_____   _____

_____   _____

Saturday

Time:

Date _____

Appointments/Notes:

_____   _____

_____   _____

_____   _____

_____   _____

_____   _____

_____   _____

Weekly Planner

Sunday   Date _____
Time: Appointments/Notes:

_____   _____

_____   _____

_____   _____

_____   _____

_____   _____

_____   _____

Monthly Calendar

Month: _____

Mon.	Tues.	Wed.	Thurs.	Fri.	Sat.	Sun.

4. **Plan a schedule with your supervisor.** You can plan for many events in your life, such as vacations or car maintenance, dental, doctor, and lawyer appointments. Your supervisor usually can schedule a one-day absence with only a few weeks' notice. A vacation may require several months' notice. Ask your supervisor how much notice you need to give to schedule days off.

5. **Call the employer.** Even the best planning won't cover all possible problems that can keep you from getting to work. An employer usually will understand if you miss work once in a while. Ask your supervisor how many days are considered reasonable to be absent from work each year. Most organizations will take disciplinary action for frequent or unexcused absences, for absences that occur a day before or after a holiday, and for not calling in or taking off to do personal business. The discipline may range from a verbal warning for the first offense to immediate discharge.[6] Call your supervisor as soon as you know you cannot get to work.

Notify Your Supervisor

When you notify your supervisor that you can't be at work, follow these steps:

- Identify yourself and say that you can't come to work.

- Explain the reason you can't be at work. *Don't lie.*

- If you expect to be gone for more than a day, tell the supervisor how long you will be away from the job.

- Express your willingness to make up the hours you missed.

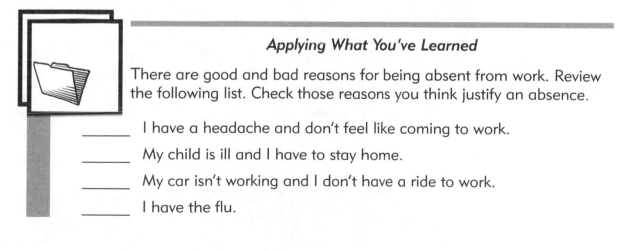

Applying What You've Learned

There are good and bad reasons for being absent from work. Review the following list. Check those reasons you think justify an absence.

_____ I have a headache and don't feel like coming to work.

_____ My child is ill and I have to stay home.

_____ My car isn't working and I don't have a ride to work.

_____ I have the flu.

_____ I have an appointment with my attorney.

_____ There's been a death in my family.

_____ My brother asked me to baby-sit his children.

_____ I had a fight with my spouse and I'm too upset to work.

_____ I sprained my ankle and need to keep it elevated.

_____ I need to visit a sick friend in the hospital.

_____ Our house was broken into last night.

_____ I need to get a new pair of glasses.

_____ I had a car accident on the way to work.

_____ It was a long weekend and I have a hangover.

_____ This is a religious holiday for me.

The Friday/Monday Syndrome

Supervisors recognize a pattern that develops among some employees. It's most common among younger workers. The syndrome becomes apparent when a worker frequently calls in sick on Fridays and Mondays. This worker is eager to start the weekend, and when Monday rolls around is either too tired or needs time off to do personal business. Even when you have a legitimate excuse, supervisors will be suspicious when most of your absences occur on Fridays and Mondays.

You should always tell the truth when you report to your supervisor. A lie may be discovered and cause you embarrassment. It will take a long time to regain your supervisor's trust if you are caught in a lie.

Getting to Work on Time

Late workers cause the same problems for an employer as absent workers. There are reasonable causes for being late; however, more than once a month or four or five times a year is considered excessive by some employers. You need to plan ahead to be on time. Here are some suggestions to help you accomplish this.

■ **Use a reliable alarm clock.** If you have an electric clock, make sure it has a back-up power source or use a wind-up clock as well in case the electricity shuts off. You can get portable or travel alarms that are battery-powered for less than an hour's wage. You can't afford to lose a job because you don't get to work on time. Don't rely on someone else to get you up.

■ **Get up early.** Allow yourself time to get ready and get to work. Plan enough time to eat breakfast and for transportation delays. You should also plan to arrive at work 8 to 10 minutes early. This cushion will help you mentally prepare for the day and reduce stress. It also shows your supervisor you are eager to work.

■ **Plan for special conditions.** There will be days when you'll need more time to get to work. For example, poor weather conditions usually slow traffic. Get up earlier so you will still arrive on time.

■ **Call your supervisor if you will be more than 15 minutes late.** You should give the following information:

— Tell why you will be late.

— Explain that you are going to get to work as soon as possible.

— Estimate when you will arrive.

— Assure your supervisor you will make up the time.

— When you get to work, apologize and make it clear it won't happen again.

Applying What You've Learned

Buster was absent for two days from his job as a production worker at a shoe factory. When he returned, his supervisor, Mr. Brown, was angry. "Why didn't you call to let me know you weren't coming to work?"

Buster was surprised and answered, "My father-in-law died and we had to attend the funeral."

Mr. Brown replied, "I'm sorry about your father-in-law, but I'm going to issue you a written warning. If this ever happens again you'll be fired."

1. Why did Mr. Brown react this way? _____

_____

_____

2. How could Buster have avoided this problem? _____

_____

_____

Vanessa went to a party on Thursday night, even though she had to be at work at 7:30 A.M. the next morning. She overslept on Friday morning and got to work 45 minutes late. Two weeks ago she went to a party on Sunday and skipped work the next day. A week ago she was 20 minutes late because she had to pick up a friend and take her to work. Her supervisor warned her then not to be late for work. When Vanessa got to the office on Friday, the receptionist told her that her supervisor wanted to see her immediately.

1. What do you think her supervisor will say? _____

   _____

   _____

2. What should Vanessa do to keep her job and avoid this situation in the future? _____

   _____

   _____

Summing Up

Reliable workers are essential to an effective operation. That's why good attendance and punctuality are important to employers. Many organizations encourage good attendance and punctuality through raises, bonuses, and promotions. A little planning and self-discipline will help you be a dependable, and valuable, worker.

Notes

1. Tom Peters, *Thriving On Chaos: Handbook for a Management Revolution* (New York: Knopf, 1987).

2. "Absenteeism on the Rise for Fourth Straight Year," *Personnel Journal* (December 1995), 21.

3. Peter G. Hanson, *Stress for Success: How to Make Stress on the Job Work for You* (New York: Doubleday, 1989).

4. Stanley Coren, *Sleep Thieves: An Eye-Opening Exploration into the Science and Mysteries of Sleep* (New York: Free Press, 1996).

5. "On the Money," *Reader's Digest* (March 1990), 17.

6. Randall Schuler and Vandra Huber, *Personnel and Human Resource Management* (St. Paul, MN: West Publishing, 1990), 345-346.

Chapter 6

What's It All About?

Knowing how to learn is probably the most critical skill for job success. You spend the early years of your life learning in school, which provides a structured approach to learning. Sometimes people think they only learn when they go to school, but humans learn in a variety of ways. We watch other people doing something and we learn. We ask other people how to do something, and we learn. We read books and magazines, and we learn. There are a number of ways we can learn besides formal schooling.

Learning Is the Key to Success

Lifelong learning is a key to success in the new labor market. Management experts today emphasize *the learning organization,* which is one that creates a climate that helps employees learn from their experiences both individually and collectively.[1] You must personally take charge of your own learning to remain a vital part of the learning organization. It's necessary to continually improve your skills to keep your job or to get a new job.[2] This chapter explores how you can be an active learner on the job.

You'll have to learn many things at your new job. But learning doesn't end once you've mastered the job. In time, your job will require new abilities, or you may want a promotion that requires additional skills.

The following exercise is designed to help you think about the many ways you can learn. As you are doing this exercise, consider how the same steps you took in your learning project could help you learn new skills at work.

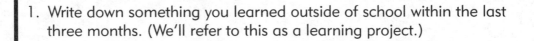

1. Write down something you learned outside of school within the last three months. (We'll refer to this as a learning project.)

   _____

   _____

   _____

2. What was the purpose or objective? (What did you set out to learn?)

   _____

   _____

   _____

   _____

3. List the steps you went through during your learning project.

   _____

   _____

   _____

   _____

4. What resources—people, reading material, computer information, and so on—did you use in the learning project?

_____

_____

_____

_____

5. Was your learning project successful? Why or why not?

_____

_____

_____

_____

6. Are there other ways you could have learned the same thing? Explain how this could have been done.

_____

_____

_____

_____

How Adults Learn

As people mature and move beyond high school, there are some common characteristics of how they learn. Adults prefer to learn using methods based on *andragogy*—a theory of adult learning.[3] Four important characteristics of adult learners are listed below.

1. **We learn better when we assume responsibility and control over learning activities.** This means you will learn more if you take charge of the learning. Don't wait for someone to teach you a new skill. Instead, seek out ways that you can learn new skills.

2. **We learn more effectively by applying what we learn.** There are progressive steps to learning. We learn the least when someone tells us how to do a task. We learn more when someone demonstrates the task. We learn the most by doing the task ourselves.

3. **As we mature, we have a broader experience base to draw on.** This experience base can be used to help us improve our learning. Compare a new task you are trying to learn with past experiences. Determine what is the same and what is different. Linking new skills and knowledge to a past experience usually improves learning.

4. **We learn better when it is clear to us why it is necessary.** In school, you may have learned something because you were going to be tested on it. On the job, your motivation to learn will be stronger when you understand the reasons for and benefits of learning a new skill.

There also are some characteristics of all learners that should help you improve your learning.

1. **The more time we spend on a learning task, the more learning takes place.** A common saying illustrates this point: *Practice makes perfect*. Spend time learning a new skill.

2. **Learning patterns differ,** so don't compare yourself to someone else trying to learn the job. Another person may excel at learning new tasks. However, as you progress on the job you may start learning faster than others. You should also recognize that some days will be better than others. This is normal, since we don't usually experience a straight line of improvement in our learning patterns. Don't let the more common, uneven pattern of learning discourage you.

3. **You can organize your learning using association.** For example, if you need to learn a list of furniture items, group them by rooms in a house. Memorize codes by associating them with a special date on the calendar, telephone numbers, addresses, or such. Many people find that memorizing facts is easier when they associate the fact with a word and make the words rhyme.

4. **When you have a more complex task to learn, use the whole-part-whole method.** This means first reviewing the task as whole, doing every part in one continuous sequence. Next, break it into small parts and concentrate on learning each part individually. Finally, practice the entire task as a whole again.

Practicing these ideas can help you become a more effective learner. You don't have to use all of them with each new learning task. In fact, some will be more useful than others, depending on what you're trying to learn. Pick out the ideas you think will help you the most in learning a task and use them.

Learning to Do Your Job

To be successful in a job you must do it correctly. This seems obvious, but it's a truth that's not always easy to follow. It's essential that you know what tasks are assigned to the job, how to perform them, and how your work will be evaluated. Let's look at how you can get this information.

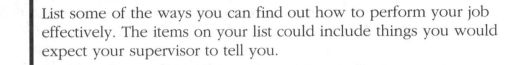

List some of the ways you can find out how to perform your job effectively. The items on your list could include things you would expect your supervisor to tell you.

_____

_____

_____

_____

Where to Find Information

Several proven methods of learning about your job are described below. Read and compare this material to your list above.

- **Job description.** This is a written profile of the job and should include all tasks and responsibilities of the job. But you will still need additional information to do your job well. Ask your supervisor to explain the job description to you. Make sure you understand your responsibilities.

- **Training.** Businesses spend almost as much money each year to train employees as elementary and high schools and colleges spend to educate students.[4] You can expect to receive some sort of training when you begin a job. There are two basic types of training:

    1. **On-the-job training.** Typically, this is one-on-one instruction that takes place as you do the job. Your supervisor or a coworker will explain what to do, show you how to do it, watch while you practice, and then tell you how well you did in practice.

    2. **Classroom instruction.** Classroom instruction involves training several employees at the same time. There are many methods used in classroom instruction, including lectures, videos, discussion, role playing, case studies, games, and learning exercises. It's important to listen carefully, ask questions when you don't understand something, and actively participate in all learning activities.

Supervisors. Managers should explain what they expect, but they may forget to tell you something. That's why it's important to ask for an explanation of your job if one is not given. While the job description explains the tasks you are to do, it doesn't give you all the details. Supervisors will help you understand exactly how the task should be done and, more importantly, how they will evaluate your performance.

Coworkers. Watch other workers who do the same job and note how they complete their tasks. They may have insight into how to do the job more easily and efficiently and how the supervisor expects the job to be done. Maybe someone was promoted from the job you have. Talk with that person. Find out how he or she did the job.

Friends. Talk with friends and acquaintances who work at jobs similar to yours. Ask them how they do their jobs. You might get some good ideas to apply to your job. However, you should talk with your supervisor before trying out any of their suggestions.

Schools. There may be classes you can take to learn more about your job. Such classes often are offered through adult education or continuing education programs at high schools or colleges. Over 40 percent of all adults participate in adult education programs.[5] Some employers will help pay the cost, because they know they will benefit from your skills. If, for example, you work with personal computers, you can probably enroll in a local computer class.

Conferences. Professional and trade associations often have conferences. You can attend these conferences and learn from the experts. You also have opportunities to meet and talk with other people who do work like yours. In addition, there are usually expositions where vendors sell the latest equipment, programs, and services related to the work. You can learn a lot from these vendors and their products. Conference registration can cost anywhere from $200 to $2,000. Talk with your coworkers to find out about the conferences they found most useful.

Workshops. Private training companies offer workshops you can attend to learn new skills. These workshops can range in cost from $100 for a day to $3,000 for a three- to five-day workshop. The quality of these workshops varies greatly. Check with coworkers and friends to find out what they know about a workshop you plan to attend. Ask the training company to supply references from people who have attended. You may want to call some of these people. Look for companies that provide a money-back guarantee.

■ **Reading.** Read about your job. General publications—like the *Dictionary of Occupational Titles, Exploring Careers,* and the *Occupational Outlook Handbook*—provide general occupational descriptions. These resources are good for workers just starting in a new occupation. Also read trade and professional magazines about your work. You should be able to find these and other occupational books and magazines in your local library.

You want to be the best worker possible, so use all the sources listed above as well as any others you can think of. Compare the resources discussed here with the steps you listed in the previous exercise.

1. List the resources you used from above.

_____   _____

_____   _____

_____   _____

_____   _____

2. What resources did you use that aren't listed in this book?

_____   _____

_____   _____

_____   _____

_____   _____

Key Definition

The Learning Organization

A learning organization is creative instead of reactive. Its growth should come from aspiration, imagination, and experimentation.[6] Another characteristic of a learning organization is a focus on cooperation instead of competition. Cooperation helps us look at what we can learn as an organization and how we can apply what we learn together. A learning organization is dynamic and growing because it changes and improves based on what it learns. As more organizations strive to become learning organizations, new principles will be identified to help them achieve this goal. You need to be an active participant in this process in any company you work for.

Applying What You've Learned

Marc has a computer technology degree from a technical school and is about to start his first job as a computer operator with a large accounting firm. He has never worked with the RISC 6000 computer, which is what the company uses. At the interview, his supervisor assured him the company will provide on-the-job training. On his first day at work, Marc's supervisor says he is too busy to work with Marc on training. Instead, he shows Marc how to back up disk drives with the high-speed tape drive. He then tells Marc to spend the rest of the day doing back-ups.

1. If you were Marc, how would you feel about this?

_____

_____

_____

_____

2. What would you do to find out more about the job you were hired to do?

_____

_____

_____

_____

Paula began working as a receptionist last week. Her supervisor told her that she is to provide clerical support for several staff members in the real estate office. This morning Susan asked her to file some house listings. While Paula was doing that, Karin asked her to type a letter. She had just started typing the letter when John told her to stop typing and immediately prepare a contract. As Paula was preparing the contract, she was interrupted by several phone calls. Karin came to get the letter and was upset because it wasn't finished. John came out of his office and began to argue with Karin, telling her to let Paula finish the contract.

1. If you were Paula, how would you feel?

_____

_____

_____

_____

2. What information does Paula need to help her in this situation? How can she get the information she needs?

_____

_____

_____

_____

Education for Life

You will always learn new things about your job. New machines may be installed. Policies and procedures may change. A new product may be manufactured and sold. The point is that all businesses are subject to change. As the business changes, so will your job. To keep up, you must understand how you learn best, and practice those techniques.

You may think your education is complete when you finish school. That is far from true. You will need to continue learning throughout your life. Futurist John Naisbitt wrote, "There is no one education, no one skill, that lasts a lifetime now."[7] Whenever you begin a new job you start learning all over again. You must learn how the organization operates and how to perform your job.

Many organizations provide ongoing training. If your employer does not provide training to keep your skills current, consider getting trained on your own. It will help you stay competitive in today's job market. In addition, it makes you more valuable. A study reported in *The Wall Street Journal* found that workers who participated in two- to five-day training courses provided by their company earned an average of 10 percent more than those who didn't.[8] *You are responsible for your lifelong education.* You can participate in company training, continuing education classes, college classes, workshops, and conferences to improve your job skills.

You will learn more when you understand your preferred method of learning. Everyone has a learning style. Your style is determined by the ways you prefer to learn something new.

In the checklist below, rank from 1 (most preferred) to 7 (least preferred) the ways you prefer to learn.

_____ **Reading:** You learn best by reading and writing.

_____ **Listening:** You learn by listening to lectures, tapes, or records.

_____ **Observing:** You learn by watching demonstrations, videos, films, or slides.

_____ **Talking:** You learn by talking with other people or through question-and-answer sessions.

_____ **Doing:** You learn best by actually doing what you are trying to learn.

_____ **Participating:** You learn by participating in games, role plays, and other activities.

_____ **Smelling/tasting:** You learn by associating what you are learning with a smell or taste.

Look at how you ranked the methods. Now list the three learning methods you like best and use most frequently.

1. _____

2. _____

3. _____

These three methods show your learning style. You may like reading and observing, or you might prefer listening and talking. You may learn by doing, participating, and smelling or tasting. Or you may use all of these senses. There are other ways to determine how you learn. Tests such as the Myers-Briggs Type Indicator can help you determine more about your learning style.[9]

It's important that you understand the ways you learn best. This can help you become a better learner. When you are faced with learning a new task, try to use your preferred learning methods. If you like *doing*, then you will not learn as well if you try to learn by *reading*. However, there are times when we must use a method not of our choosing. When this happens, do your best to use the required method and try to use your preferred style to review what you have learned.

Steps to Learning

Although everyone has his or her own learning style, there are some specific steps you can take to improve the way you learn. At the beginning of this chapter, you completed an exercise on something you recently learned outside of school. This was called your learning project. The term *learning project* simply means the process of learning something new. The steps to complete a learning project are explained below. You probably listed some of them earlier.

1. **Motivate yourself.** You must find something exciting or interesting about your learning project. If you aren't interested in the subject itself, you might be interested in something that could result from what you learn. For example, learning to fill out a new form required for your job may not excite you, but you might get excited about receiving a raise because you do such a good job of completing the form. Write down your reasons for wanting to complete a learning project before you start the process.

2. **Set objectives.** The final outcomes of learning are called objectives. You need to know your learning objectives. Ask yourself the following question to identify these: "When I am done with this learning project, what must I be able to do?" Write down these objectives. Be specific, and state what you want to be able to do when the learning project is completed.

3. **Identify resources.** Find out what resources are available to help you reach your learning objectives. These resources may come from several areas, including these:

    ■ **In-house learning opportunities.** Ask your supervisor if your company offers any courses that can help you meet your learning objectives. Perhaps there is another worker who can teach you what you want to learn.

    ■ **Outside education.** Ask someone in your organization (a training manager, human resources manager, personnel director, or supervisor) to help you learn about courses offered at vocational schools, community colleges, universities, and specialized training firms in your community.

    ■ **Additional methods.** Discuss your learning needs with friends and coworkers. Find out what methods they have used to learn something similar. Ask what kinds of books, videotapes, or audio tapes are available at your library. Also, check the Internet for information.

4. **Choose the best resources.** Which of the resources you identify will help you the most in completing your learning project? You may decide to use more than one resource. Another factor to consider is cost. Find out if your employer will pay for any of these resources, and if you will be allowed to take time from work to pursue your learning objective. Also keep in mind that other people are an important resource for any learning project.[10]

5. **Schedule the project.** Once you select the resources you will use, plan the time needed for your project and decide when you want to complete it. If you need to take time from work for this, discuss the matter with your supervisor.

6. **Write down questions.** Decide what questions you need to answer to learn the task. Write the questions on a piece of paper. Check them off as you find the answers. Questions should ask who, what, where, when, why, and how.

7. **Complete the project.** Completing any learning project requires self-discipline. You must follow through with the plan you create. It might be helpful to find someone who will keep you on track by checking your progress.

8. **Evaluate progress.** As you complete the learning project, evaluate your progress. Are the resources you decided to use providing you with the knowledge and skills you need? Are you following the schedule you set? Are you meeting your objectives? Have an experienced person test your new skills and knowledge. Remember, the most important step to successful learning is accomplishing your objectives.

9. **Practice.** The most effective way to become more skilled is to practice what you've learned even after the learning project is complete. Periodically check yourself on how well you can apply your new knowledge.

Personal Learning Project

This exercise is designed to help you put into practice the steps needed to complete a learning project.

1. Select a skill you want to learn and write it below.

_____

2. What is your motivation? Why do you want to learn this skill? How do you think you will feel after you learn it?

_____

_____

_____

_____

3. Decide on a learning objective. What are your expected outcomes?

_____

_____

_____

_____

4. Who can help you plan your learning project?

_____

_____

_____

_____

5. What resources can you use to complete your learning project?

_____

_____

_____

_____

6. What do you think will be your best resource? Keep in mind your learning style, cost, availability, etc.

_____

_____

_____

7. When would you like to complete the learning project?

_____

_____

_____

_____

8. How much time will you spend daily or weekly on the project?

_____

_____

_____

_____

9. How will you evaluate your progress?

_____

_____

_____

_____

10. How will you practice what you learn?

_____

_____

_____

_____

Applying What You've Learned

The ability to learn is the most important skill you can have. Successful people know how to learn new things. Read the following case studies and develop a plan for each person to learn a new skill. Be specific about the steps for each learning project. Use more paper if necessary.

Donna has spent the last four months working at the Quick Print Shop. She runs a copy machine for orders of 500 or fewer copies. Donna has decided she would like to learn more about graphic arts. She'd like to be able to run the offset press used for larger orders and those requiring more complex printing techniques.

1. What should Donna do to learn this new skill?

_____

_____

_____

_____

_____

Juan works as a bank teller. He would like to work in the accounting department, where he could earn a higher salary. If he knew more about accounting, he would have a better chance at a promotion to that area.

1. What should Juan do to learn more about accounting?

_____

_____

_____

_____

_____

Summing Up

On-the-job learning is an important skill to master. Training you receive on the job accounts for 85 percent of the earnings differential among workers.[11] Taking advantage of such training makes you more valuable to your employer. Keep in mind that there will be many times you must learn on your own. The more you practice learning, the better your learning skills will be.

Notes

1. Dave Ulrich, Mary Von Glinow, and Todd Jick, "High-Impact Learning: Building and Diffusing Learning Capability," *Organizational Dynamics* (Month, 1993), 52.

2. Derwin Fox, "Career Insurance for Today's World," *Training & Development* (March 1996), 61.

3. Malcolm Knowles, *The Adult Learner: A Neglected Species* (Houston, TX: Gulf Publishing, 1984).

4. Anthony Carnevale, Leila Gainer, and Janice Villet, *Training in America* (San Francisco: Jossey-Bass, 1990).

5. U.S. Department of Education, "Participation in Adult Education." In *The Condition of Education, 1996.* (Washington, DC: Government Printing Office, 1996).

6. Joseph H. Boyett, with Jimmie T. Boyett, *Beyond Workplace 2000* (New York: Dutton, 1995).

7. John Naisbitt and Patricia Aburdene, *Reinventing the Corporation,* (New York: Warner Books, 1985).

8. Work Week, "Training Pays," *The Wall Street Journal* (May 7, 1996), A1.

9. Gordon Lawrence, *People Types and Tiger Stripes: A Practical Guide to Learning Styles*, 3rd Edition (Gainesville, FL: Center for Applications of Psychological Type, 1993).

10. H. K. Morris Baskett, "Advice to the Learnlorn," *Training & Development* (March 1994), p. 61.

11. *Serving the New Corporation* (Alexandria, VA: American Society for Training and Development, 1986).

Chapter 7

Knowing Yourself

According to research, employers want employees with positive self-concepts.[1] Higher morale, more motivation, and greater productivity are indications of a positive self-concept. Because productivity, work quality, creativity, and flexibility are based on self-concept, a positive self-concept affects your job success.

To be a good employee, you must believe you are a good employee. In other words, you must have confidence in your abilities. Your confidence comes from your self-concept, which is a mixture of your self-image (how you see yourself) and self-esteem (how you feel about your self-image). Let's look at how these affect the way you approach a job.

Your Self-Concept Can Make You or Break You

Have you ever known a woman who really wasn't a great beauty, but because she acted as if she were beautiful, other people believed she was? A positive self-image can turn an ugly duckling into a beautiful swan. On the other hand, beautiful swans with poor self-images often go unnoticed and unappreciated their entire lives.

Your self-image is influenced by many people. Parents influence how you view yourself. Many adults admit they still feel an urge to "please Mom and Dad." Your brothers and sisters often are your most willing critics. Teachers and supervisors evaluate you. You may feel a certain grade is a statement of your personal worth. Peers influence how you act, what you wear, and even where you go.

The good news is that the single most important influence on your self-image is *you*. How you feel about any facet of yourself makes up your self-esteem. You can't be negative unless you choose to be negative. By learning to know and value yourself, you can choose to have a positive self-image.

A positive self-concept is reflected in your work relationships. The ability to communicate with your supervisor, coworkers, and customers is extremely important. If you do not view yourself in a positive way, these relationships will be hindered. In this chapter we'll explore ways you can improve your self-awareness and create a positive self-concept.

Applying What You've Learned

Corey has been working after school at the Speedi-In Deli for a year. His job involves stocking shelves, keeping the pop machines filled, and general clean-up chores. Corey works fairly independently. He enjoys his job, but feels he would like to advance to a behind-the-counter job. Although Corey doesn't have a positive self-image, he believes he could do this job.

The deli manager is pleased with Corey's work. On Friday, he puts a note in Corey's pay envelope: "Great job! Looking forward to advancing you."

On Monday, Corey and the manager are the only people working in the stockroom. The manager doesn't say anything about the note, but seems to be expecting a response from Corey. Because Corey doesn't feel good about himself, he feels uncomfortable accepting the manager's praise. He doesn't know what to say.

1. How will Corey's manager react if Corey doesn't say anything?

   _____

   _____

   _____

2. Will this affect Corey's opportunity for promotion to a counter job? Explain your answer.

   _____

   _____

   _____

3. How will your answer to question 2 affect Corey's self-concept?

   _____

   _____

   _____

Dani had a speech problem as a young child. She was often teased because of it. Speech therapy in elementary school helped Dani overcome her handicap. Although she no longer has the speech problem, Dani is not confident in social conversations. She doesn't look at people when she talks, and sometimes she mumbles.

Dani works at the Burger Bash as a fry cook. She spends her entire shift in the kitchen, and she would like another job at the restaurant. Dani knows that one of the cashiers is quitting at the end of the school year to attend college. She really wants the cashier's job, but she's afraid her poor communication skills will hinder her chance of promotion.

Dani decides to overcome this obstacle. At first, she practices simple conversations with friends and coworkers. She even makes a special effort to talk to some of her teachers and an elderly neighbor. She also takes a public speaking course at school. When her Burger Bash supervisor has team meetings, Dani answers questions and even jokes with the group. Gradually, she feels better about talking in social situations.

1. How will Dani's actions affect her chances of becoming a cashier?

   _____

   _____

   _____

2. How is Dani's self-concept affected by her actions? Explain the reason for your answer.

_____

_____

_____

Difficulties in the workplace create job stress. Not only will your job be more enjoyable if you approach it in a positive way, you will reduce your job stress. This positive approach begins with a positive self-image, which enhances your confidence to do the job. After all, your employer hired you because he or she believes you are qualified to do the work. Your employer believes in you.

Learn to Believe in Yourself

Sometimes it may seem like everyone at work knows what they are doing except you. That's not true. No one always feels confident. Anyone can experience a poor self-image, especially when circumstances change abruptly. For example:

- A teacher loses her job because there's no money to fund the gifted program for the coming year. She questions her ability to find a new teaching position. She wants to try a new area of work, but wonders if she's really qualified to enter a new field. Her indecision is caused by a sudden lack of confidence.

- A man is laid off after working 23 years in the same manufacturing plant. Rumors spread that the plant will soon close and move to a new location. Questions run through his mind: "Should I move my family to the new plant location? Should I start that auto repair shop I've always dreamed about? What if I can't pay all the bills?" He has trouble deciding what to do.

- Your supervisor is asked to move up in the company. She currently has 10 employees reporting to her. She will be responsible for 50 workers if she accepts the new position. The hours are the same and the pay is better. But she'll have to take a computer course at the local university to work in the new area. She begins to question her abilities: "Can I handle a college course? I haven't attended a university class in 10 years. What if I can't pass the course? What if I can't operate the computer? Can I really supervise 50 people? Maybe I'm not ready for a promotion just yet."

Having a positive self-concept doesn't mean you won't ever question yourself. In fact, the questions these people asked are healthy. Questioning allows you to compare your self-image with the world around you. You don't want to put yourself in a position where you can't perform well because you inaccurately evaluated your skills and abilities. This is why self-awareness is so important. It allows you to make better decisions about your career and how to perform on a job.

Take Control of Your Life

According to scientists who study personalities, people approach life in one of two ways: They either feel they control their own lives or they feel that other people and things control them.[2] The way you look at life greatly affects your self-concept. The following quiz will help you understand how you view your control over your life.

Answer the following questions. Put a **T** beside the statements you think are true and an **F** beside those you think are false.

Your Approach to Life Quiz

Views of life	Answer	Score
1. Other people control my life.	_____	_____
2. I am responsible for the success in my life.	_____	_____
3. Success in life is a matter of luck.	_____	_____
4. When things go wrong, it's usually because of things I couldn't control.	_____	_____
5. The last time I did something successful, I knew it was successful because of my own efforts.	_____	_____
6. The last time I failed at something, I knew it was because I just wasn't good enough to get the job done.	_____	_____

7. Most successful people are born successful. _____ _____

8. It seems that most things are beyond my control. _____ _____

9. When I fail, it's usually someone else's fault. _____ _____

10. When I succeed, it is usually because of someone else's efforts. _____ _____

Score: _____ *Total Score:* _____

Scoring:

Statement 1: True = 0, False = 1   Statement 6: True = 0, False = 1
Statement 2: True = 1, False = 0   Statement 7: True = 0, False = 1
Statement 3: True = 0, False = 1   Statement 8: True = 0, False = 1
Statement 4: True = 0, False = 1   Statement 9: True = 0, False = 1
Statement 5: True = 1, False = 0   Statement 10: True = 0, False = 1

Your Score and Your View of Life

■ **0 - 3 = Outside My Control:** *I'm not responsible for my successes or my failures.* I need to work on my self-concept.

■ **4 - 6 = Sometimes in Control:** *I'm sometimes responsible for my successes and failures.* My self-concept could be improved.

■ **7 - 10 = In Control:** *I'm responsible for my successes.* I have confidence in myself and have a good self-concept.

Learn to View Life Positively

People with positive self-concepts look at their successes and believe they are responsible for them. They also believe that, while they are responsible for their failures, events, things, and people outside their control also affect the outcome. People with negative self-concepts view the world in the opposite way. They credit their successes to luck and never accept the blame for their failures. Thus, they fail to accept responsibility for their own actions. Those in the *Outside My Control* category in the quiz need to work harder to develop a positive self-concept, while those in the *In Control* category find it easier to develop a positive self-concept.

Like anything else, this approach to life can be taken to extremes. There are times when your success is due to luck and failure is solely your own fault. But by being realistic about your personal contributions to success and failure, you'll know how to improve yourself. Most important, *you must believe you can improve.* In fact, you can overcome any problem or difficulty given enough time, effort, and, when needed, help from other people. The important thing is to have faith in yourself.

You can teach yourself to view life more positively and to be in control of your own life.[3] Look at the circumstances every time you succeed. Give yourself credit for your success. Remember to look at the small successes that occur every day of your life. Similarly, when you experience failure, examine the reasons for it. Look for those outside factors that contributed to the failure and realize how they affected the outcome. In the next exercise, you will look at the successes and failures in your life and see how you personally contribute to your successes.

Selling Yourself on You

Joe Girard was the best car salesman in the world for eight years in a row, selling more than 11,200 cars. He was successful because he believed in himself. In the book *How to Sell Yourself*, he gave these tips for improving self-image.[4]

- Tell yourself you are number one every morning.
- Write "I believe in myself" on cards and place them where you'll see them frequently throughout the day.
- Associate with other winners and avoid losers.
- Put negative thoughts—like envy, jealousy, greed, and hate—out of your life.
- Pat yourself on the back at least once a day.
- Repeat "I will" at least 10 times each day.
- Do the things you fear most to prove you can successfully accomplish them.

Personal Evaluation Exercise

1. List three successes you had during the past week.

_____

_____

_____

2. How were you responsible for making each success happen?

_____

_____

_____

3. List three failures you had during the past week.

_____

_____

_____

4. Describe outside factors that contributed to each failure.

_____

_____

_____

There are some important things to learn from this exercise. First, we all have successes in our lives. You should take the credit and reward yourself for them. Second, we all have failures in our lives, but every failure can be overcome. Analyze the reasons for failure. Was it really your fault, or was it the result of something you couldn't anticipate? Look at failure as an opportunity to learn from mistakes and avoid repeating them in the future. As you apply these principles in your life you can learn to take control and develop a more positive self-concept.

1. What can you learn from each of your successes?

_____

_____

_____

2. What can you learn from each of your failures?

_____

_____

_____

Self-Concept in the Workplace

There will be experiences in your life that will make you doubt yourself. A positive self-image helps overcome doubt about your abilities. You face unique challenges in the work world. Many job-related situations are totally new to you. For instance, if you're starting a new job you may question your ability to complete your assigned tasks. But it's important to remember that self-confidence increases as you gain experience. To protect your positive self-image as you begin a new job, try to remember these two simple truths:

1. **You will make mistakes.** When you make mistakes, acknowledge them. Accept any criticism or advice from your supervisor and correct the mistake. For each mistake, examine the situation and note the contributing factors. Decide how you can avoid the same mistake in the future. This way you learn from your mistakes. You're capable of improving your self-image by learning from past mistakes—and not blaming yourself.

2. **Your employer wants you to succeed.** Employers don't hire people in order to fire them. Your employer hired you because of your skills, because he or she believes you have the ability to do the job successfully. Give yourself credit for your accomplishments. Learn to accept compliments gracefully. When you are complimented on your work, simply say, "Thank you." If your supervisor or coworkers neglect to compliment you, compliment yourself!

I Believe in Me!

Self-confidence is a belief in yourself and in your abilities. It is vital for your success. All great leaders have this quality. It doesn't mean you won't have periods of doubt—particularly when you experience a failure. It does mean that you look within yourself to discover how to overcome failures. Keep in mind that you are special and unique. No one else is quite like you. No one can contribute the same qualities to a job that you can. Learn to appreciate who you are.

Identify Your Skills

Take an honest look at yourself. You may be surprised at the variety of skills you have to offer an employer. You develop skills from all your life experiences. Many of the exercises in this section are adapted from *Getting the Job You Really Want,* by J. Michael Farr.[5] They're designed to help you become aware of your skills, which are divided into three categories:

◼ Self-management or adaptive skills

◼ Transferable skills

◼ Job-related skills

Self-Management Skills

Self-management skills are related to the control you have over your life: how you plan, implement, change, and evaluate the activities in your life. Some self-management skills are necessary to please your employer. You probably have some of these skills already. Your employer expects you to use these skills most of the time. While not all employers look for the same skills, the key self-management skills listed here are highly valued by all employers.

Self-Management Skills Checklist

Check the most appropriate column for all the following skills that apply to you. These are skills all employers value highly. Employers often will not hire a person who does not have or use most or all of these.

Key Self-Management Skills	Usually	Sometimes
Employers values workers who …		
get to work every day		
arrive on time		
get things done		
follow instructions from supervisors		
get along well with coworkers		
are honest		
work hard		
ability to ask questions		
ability to complete assignments		
ability to handle responsibility		
ability to learn quickly		
ambition		
assertiveness		
creativity		
dependability		
enthusiasm		
flexibility		
friendliness		
good sense of humor		
high motivation		
intelligence		
leadership		
maturity		
patience		
persistence		
physical strength		
pride in doing a good job		

Other Self-Management Skills	Usually	Sometimes
problem-solving ability	_____	_____
results-oriented approach	_____	_____
self-motivation	_____	_____
sincerity	_____	_____
willingness to learn new things	_____	_____
_____	_____	_____
_____	_____	_____
_____	_____	_____
_____	_____	_____
_____	_____	_____
_____	_____	_____
_____	_____	_____

Review the charts you just filled out. Count the number of times you checked *Usually* and *Sometimes*. Record the numbers below.

Self-Management Skills Record

Usually: _____

Sometimes: _____

Total Skill Points: _____

Transferable Skills

Transferable skills can be used in many different jobs. A grocery store cashier needs to understand numbers, but so do bank tellers and accounting clerks. A nurse needs good people skills, as does a receptionist or a salesperson. Employers value some transferable skills over others. The key transferable skills listed here may help you get a higher-paying job or a more responsible position, or both.

Transferable Skills Checklist

Key Transferable Skills	Usually	Sometimes
accept responsibility	_____	_____
increase sales or efficiency	_____	_____
manage money, budgets	_____	_____
manage people	_____	_____
meet deadlines	_____	_____
meet the public	_____	_____
organize and manage projects	_____	_____
plan	_____	_____
solve problems	_____	_____
speak in public	_____	_____
supervise others	_____	_____
understand and control budgets	_____	_____

Tactile Skills	Usually	Sometimes
assemble	_____	_____
build	_____	_____
construct/repair things	_____	_____
drive/operate vehicles	_____	_____
good with hands	_____	_____
make things	_____	_____
observe/inspect	_____	_____
operate tools, machines	_____	_____
repair	_____	_____
use complex equipment	_____	_____

117

Data Skills	Usually	Sometimes
analyze data		
audit records		
budget		
calculate/compute		
check for accuracy		
classify data		
compare		
compile		
count		
detail-oriented		
evaluate		
investigate		
keep financial records		
locate answers or information		
manage money		
negotiate		
observe/inspect		
record facts		
research		
synthesize		
take inventory		

People Skills	Usually	Sometimes
administer		
care for		
confront others		
counsel people		
demonstrate		
diplomatic		
help others		
insightful		
instruct		
interview people		
kind		

listen	_____	_____
mentoring	_____	_____
outgoing	_____	_____
patient	_____	_____
persuade	_____	_____
pleasant	_____	_____
sensitive	_____	_____
sociable	_____	_____
supervise	_____	_____
tactful	_____	_____
teach	_____	_____
tolerant	_____	_____
tough	_____	_____
trust	_____	_____
understand	_____	_____

Using Words and Ideas Skills	Usually	Sometimes
articulate	_____	_____
communicate verbally	_____	_____
correspond with others	_____	_____
create new ideas	_____	_____
design	_____	_____
edit	_____	_____
ingenious	_____	_____
inventive	_____	_____
library research	_____	_____
logical	_____	_____
public speaking	_____	_____
remember information	_____	_____
write clearly	_____	_____

119

Leadership Skills	Usually	Sometimes
arrange social functions		
competitive		
decisive		
delegate		
direct others		
explain things to others		
mediate problems		
motivate people		
negotiate agreements		
plan		
results-oriented		
risk taker		
run meetings		
self-confident		
self-motivated		
solve problems		

Creative/Artistic Skills	Usually	Sometimes
artistic		
dance, body movement		
drawing, art		
expressive		
perform, act		
present artistic ideas		

Office/Technical Skills	Usually	Sometimes
Access and retrieve data from the Internet		
Arm/disarm security system		
Create electronic databases		
Create electronic spreadsheets		
Create multimedia presentations		
Create overhead transparencies		
Create programs using a computer language		
Operate a slide projector		
Operate copy machine		
Operate fax machine		
Operate laminator		
Operate multi-line telephone system		
Operate paper folder		
Operate paper shredder		
Operate postage meter		
Operate video recorder/player		
Use database software		
Use e-mail		
Use large screen projector		
Use overhead projector		
Use presentation software		
Use spreadsheet software		
Use word processing software		
Others_____		
_____		
_____		
_____		
_____		
_____		
_____		
_____		

Review the charts you filled out. Count the number of time you checked *Usually* and *Sometimes*. Record the numbers below.

Transferable Skills Record

Usually: _____

Sometimes: _____

Total Skill Points: _____

Job-Related Skills

You use job-related skills to do a particular job. For example, a truck driver must know how to drive a large truck and operate its gears. A paramedic must be able to take blood pressure and use a stethoscope. Some job-related skills are the result of years of training. Others may be learned in a short time.

If you are interested in a particular job, you probably have some skills necessary to do that job. These skills come from a variety of experiences including education, other jobs, volunteer work, hobbies, extracurricular activities, and even family activities. Do the following exercise to see what skills you have that could be used in the job you want.

Job-Related Skills Checklist

1. List the skills related to this job that you have gained from school courses or vocational training.

_____   _____

_____   _____

_____   _____

2. List the skills related to this job that you gained from other jobs or from volunteer work.

_____   _____

_____   _____

_____   _____

3. List the skills related to this job that you gained from hobbies, family activities, extracurricular activities, and other experiences outside of school or work.

_____ _____

_____ _____

_____ _____

■ Give yourself one point for each job-related skill you listed. Record that number below.

Total Job-Related Skills: _____

A Review of Your Skills

Add your total points for each skill area and write them in the appropriate spaces below. This shows you the variety of skills you have to offer an employer. You are a valuable member of your employer's team!

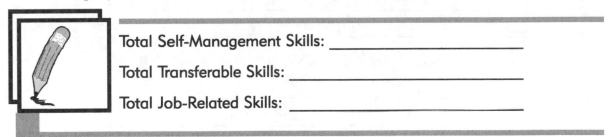

Total Self-Management Skills: _____

Total Transferable Skills: _____

Total Job-Related Skills: _____

Identifying your skills shows your strengths as an employee. Now that you know your skills, you can use them to improve your position in the work world. Is there a skill you aren't using? Do you have a skill that is weak? How could you improve this skill?

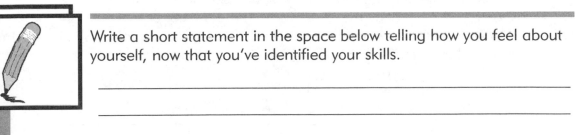

Write a short statement in the space below telling how you feel about yourself, now that you've identified your skills.

_____

_____

_____

_____

_____

Applying What You've Learned

Darren works in a formal-wear store. Last week a wedding party of 10 came in to be measured for tuxedoes. Darren carefully measured each person and recorded the measurements on the proper form. When the groom became impatient with the long wait, Darren joked with him about the wedding. By the time the group left, the groom was smiling. Then Darren discovered that he had undercharged the group by $50.

1. What are Darren's stronger skills?

    _____

    _____

    _____

2. What are Darren's weaker skills?

    _____

    _____

    _____

3. How can Darren improve his weaker skills?

    _____

    _____

    _____

Sheila works in the university research library. A professor sent a list of research articles to be reserved for his classes. Sheila went through the stacks and pulled all but one of the requested articles. Although she was unable to find one article, she packaged the rest and sent them to the professor. Her supervisor did not okay the order. Later, the professor complained to Sheila's supervisor that his order was incomplete. The supervisor called Sheila into the office and explained the mistake. Sheila became angry and left the office.

1. What are Sheila's stronger skills?

    _____

    _____

    _____

2. What are Sheila's weaker skills?

_____

_____

_____

3. How can Sheila improve her weaker skills?

_____

_____

_____

Summing Up

Dietitians tell us "You are what you eat," to encourage us to develop healthy bodies through good nutrition. To develop a healthier self-image, an appropriate saying might be "You are what you think." In truth, if you believe you can do the job, you can do it. Here are some useful tips to help you believe in yourself.

- **Think positive.** Think success, not failure. Be your own cheerleader.

- **Accept compliments.** Learn to say a simple "Thank you" when you are complimented.

- **Accept responsibility.** Learn to accept responsibility for your successes as well as your failures, but recognize how other factors contribute to failure. Be proud of your successes. Strive to improve your weaker skills and correct your mistakes.

- **Identify your skills.** Use your special abilities to improve your skills and to build up your positive self-concept.

- **Reward yourself.** Treat yourself for being successful. Buy something special to remember the occasion. Celebrate!

Notes

1. Anthony Carnevale, Leila Gainer, and Ann Meltzer, *Work Place Basics: The Essential Skills Employers Want* (San Francisco: Jossey-Bass, 1990), 215-232.

2. Richard Daft and Richard Steers, *Organizations: A Micro/Macro Approach* (Glenview, IL: Scott, Foresman, 1986), 72.

3. David Cherrington, Nyal McMullin, and Betty McMullin, *Organizational Behavior* (Boston: Allyn & Bacon, 1989), 106.

4. Joe Girard, *How to Sell Yourself* (New York: Warner Books, 1979).

5. J. Michael Farr, *Getting the Job You Really Want* (Indianapolis: JIST, 1995).

Chapter 8

Getting Along with Your Supervisor

According to management expert Martin Broadwell, supervision is getting a job done through other people.[1] This means your supervisor not only wants but needs your cooperation to get the work done.

Your supervisor may or may not be the person who hired you. However, the supervisor makes the decisions about your work and what you do. Supervisors frequently make recommendations about promotions, salary increases, and firing employees. It is important for you to get along with your supervisor. Cooperating will make your work experience more pleasant and help advance your career. It also helps you get a positive recommendation should you look for another job.

The Team Leader

In today's business world the supervisor is seen as a leader, coach, cheerleader, teacher, and counselor. This person plans, schedules, orders work materials, directs the activities of employees, checks the productivity and quality of work, and coordinates all work activities with other areas of the organization. Many organizations now use the term *team leader* instead of supervisor. The team leader often shares the responsibilities of a supervisor with other members of the team. The term *supervisor* is more traditional and still used frequently, and we'll use it in this book.

Consider yourself part of a team if you participate in a work group. Each worker must do his or her job correctly for the team to be successful. The supervisor delegates work to the members of the group. Your supervisor depends on you to do your job and to do it right.

Delegate

Supervisors assign or distribute tasks to employees. When they do the work themselves rather than delegating, their performance slips.[2] A supervisor must delegate tasks to employees in order to ensure all the work gets done. When a task is delegated to you, be sure to follow instructions carefully. Periodically, report back to your supervisor to let him or her know how the job is progressing. Let your supervisor know when you are finished with an assigned task.

What Does a Supervisor Do?

Complete this exercise to test your understanding of the responsibilities of a typical supervisor. Place an **A** beside those tasks you think a supervisor would *Always* do, an **S** beside those a supervisor would *Sometimes* do, and an **N** beside those tasks a supervisor would *Never* do.

Matt is the owner-manager of a 24-hour self-service gas station. What is Matt responsible for?

_____	Ordering gasoline	_____	Training new employees
_____	Making out the payroll	_____	Arranging for police protection
_____	Scheduling workers	_____	Pumping gas
_____	Changing oil	_____	Dismissing unacceptable employees

Why did you rate these tasks the way you did?

_____

_____

_____

Krista is the supervisor of the make-up department in a local drug store. What is Krista responsible for?

____	Ordering make-up	____	Balancing the cash register
____	Handling customer complaints	____	Evaluating employees
		____	Demonstrating products
____	Stocking the shelves	____	Returning damaged products
____	Distributing employee paychecks		

Why did you rate these tasks the way you did?

_____

_____

_____

Joel supervises a group of 15 telemarketing operators. What is Joel responsible for?

____	Settling employee disagreements	____	Solving problems
____	Scheduling vacations	____	Making phone calls
____	Listening to phone calls made by employees	____	Repairing electronic equipment
		____	Answering customer questions
____	Tracking sales		

Why did you rate these tasks the way you did?

_____

_____

_____

129

Marta is a line supervisor of an electronic components assembly factory. What is Marta responsible for?

_____ Checking quality of finished items

_____ Filling in for absent workers

_____ Setting personnel policies

_____ Keeping a parts inventory

_____ Signing employees' paychecks

_____ Evaluating worker performance

_____ Inspecting for safety violations

_____ Talking with union leaders

Why did you rate these tasks the way you did?

_____

_____

_____

Jeff manages a frozen yogurt shop. What is Jeff responsible for?

_____ Creating new yogurt flavors

_____ Taking customer orders

_____ Maintaining equipment

_____ Cleaning tables

_____ Bookkeeping

_____ Conducting health department inspections

_____ Planning advertising

_____ Making bank deposits

Why did you rate these tasks the way you did?

_____

_____

_____

It's Not an Easy Job

An old folk tale tells the story of a husband and wife who traded jobs for a day. Each thought he or she could do the other person's job better and more efficiently. Each planned an afternoon of leisure after a morning of efficient work.

The husband stayed home to do household chores, and his wife went off to the field. Neither did the other's job well. By the end of the day, the house was in total ruin, the dinner was burned, the cow was not milked, and the field was not plowed. Totally exhausted after a frustrating day, they shared a cold dinner and agreed that neither job was easy. The next day they returned to their own work with much relief.

Some employees think supervising is easy. It's important to realize that supervisors have responsibilities other employees don't have. Employees often are unaware of the stress many supervisors carry. Your supervisor's outlook of the workday may be affected by this stress. Throughout this chapter we'll look at getting along with your supervisor and helping him or her do an effective job.

Good "Followership"

Scores of books have been written about leadership. Workers are encouraged to become leaders. However, most of us will be followers for much of our lives. For this reason, the advice provided by U.S. Air Force Colonel Phillip Meilinger on *followership* is important and quite relevent.[3] His 10 principles of good followership are listed below.

1. Don't blame the boss.

2. Don't fight the boss.

3. Use initiative.

4. Accept responsibility.

5. Tell the truth and don't quibble.

6. Do your homework.

7. Be willing to implement suggestions you make.

8. Keep the boss informed.

9. Fix problems as they occur.

10. Put in an honest day's work.

Communicate with Your Supervisor

Good communication with your supervisor is important to both of you. There are five important aspects to remember when communicating with your supervisor:

1. You must be able to follow instructions.

2. You need to know how to ask questions.

3. You should report any problems and results of your work.

4. You should accurately record and give messages to your supervisor.

5. You need to discuss your job performance.

Following instructions is important at all times, but especially during your training period. Your supervisor will be watching to see how well you do this. Use your senses to follow instructions correctly.

- **Concentrate.** Focus your attention on the supervisor. Don't be distracted by noise and movement.

- **Listen.** Pay attention to the words being spoken. If you hear unfamiliar words or terms, ask for clarification. Listening also means interpreting body language, voice inflections, and gestures. If this nonverbal communication is confusing, ask the supervisor to clarify what you don't understand.

- **Watch.** Sometimes a supervisor demonstrates how a task is performed. If necessary, ask the supervisor to repeat the process until you understand it completely. Sometimes a task may be too complex or time-consuming to demonstrate. In such cases, you probably will receive general instructions. If there are details you don't understand, ask for guidance to continue the task.

- **Question.** After you have listened and watched, ask questions. A good supervisor will encourage you to ask questions. It's better to ask a question than to make a mistake because you didn't understand.

- **Write.** Write down in a small notebook the important points to remember about the instructions you get. Don't write while your supervisor is talking or demonstrating something. Do it at a break in the instructions.

- **Practice.** With your supervisor's permission, perform the task. Make sure you have fully completed the job. This may include putting tools away or cleaning up your work area. Don't leave your work partially completed.

Key Definition

Jargon

Every organization develops its own terminology. This language is called *jargon*. Jargon might be the most difficult thing for a new employee to learn. It can be in the form of words or acronyms. For example, your supervisor may tell you that you will be "pulling" today. This could mean you'll be taking packages off a conveyor belt to be loaded onto a truck. An *acronym* is an abbreviation of a phrase. If your supervisor says you can't get a computer until you submit an RFP, that may refer to "Request for Purchase." When you hear a term that is unclear, don't be afraid to ask for an explanation. Some organizations give new employees a booklet that defines terms unique to that business.

Understand Instructions

■ Take a blank sheet of 8½" by 11" paper.

■ Fold the paper in half.

■ Now fold the paper in half again.

■ Fold the paper in half one more time.

There are four possibilities that result from following these directions:

1. Your paper could measure 2-3/4" by 4-1/4".

2. Your paper could measure 2-1/4" by 5-1/2".

3. Your paper could measure 1" by 11".

4. Your paper could measure 1-3/8".

The results differ because the instructions are not entirely clear, just as some instructions you receive from a supervisor may not be completely clear.

1. What questions could you have asked to better understand the instructions?

_____

_____

_____

2. How would you rewrite the instructions so there is only one possible outcome?

_____

_____

_____

Ask Questions

If you don't understand something, ask questions. Your supervisor can't read your mind. It's better to ask a question than to make a major mistake. Yet most people are reluctant to ask questions for fear of looking stupid. If this applies to you, you need to overcome your reluctance. Not asking questions could result in broken equipment, an angry customer, or other mistakes that will negatively affect your performance rating. It may even cost you the job. Here are some simple guidelines for asking questions.

- **Ask immediately.** You should ask the question as soon as it arises. The longer you wait, the more irrelevant it will seem and you won't ask it at all.

- **Summarize the response.** When the supervisor answers your question, repeat the answer in your own words. This lets you make sure you clearly understand the answer.

- **Memorize the answer.** It's irritating to answer the same question repeatedly. Your supervisor may grow impatient with you if this happens. Record answers in a notebook if you have trouble remembering them.

Report the Results

Your supervisor needs to be kept informed of your work. Sometimes the supervisor will be close enough to observe your work at all times, but this is not always the case. It is *your* responsibility to keep the supervisor informed about your progress on a task. Contact your supervisor in the following situations.

- **When you complete a task.** The supervisor needs to know if the job has been completed. If you don't report back, he or she will have to find you to ask if the job is complete. A busy supervisor doesn't have time to track down every employee to see if they have completed their assigned tasks.

▓ **When you aren't sure how to proceed.** There will be times when you won't know how to complete a task. Whenever you don't know what to do, ask your supervisor. Remember the answer so you'll know how to handle a similar situation in the future.

▓ **When you have a problem.** Problems can develop when you are trying to complete a task. The less experience you have, the more difficult it will be to solve the problem. Equipment may not work properly. Customers may have questions you can't answer. Someone else may not have done a job right and it keeps you from finishing your assignment. When you aren't sure how to solve the problem, contact your supervisor immediately. This will keep the problem from getting worse.

Some tasks may take you several hours, days, or weeks to complete. Keep your supervisor informed about ongoing assignments. This tells your supervisor that you are assuming responsibility and that he or she can trust you. It's important for your supervisor to know he or she can rely on you to complete an assignment.

Coaching Your Job Performance

Your supervisor should communicate with you frequently about your job performance. Ken Blanchard and Don Shula have written a book about the importance of coaching workers to do their best.[4] Coaching techniques should include periodic encouragement and feedback about ways to improve your work. Receiving suggestions on improving your work may seem like a negative experience. But it's better than losing your job. Coaching helps you do a better job for your organization. Here are some simple guidelines to help you communicate effectively with your supervisor about your job performance.

▓ **Don't respond to feedback with anger.** Feedback from your supervisor is important. No one enjoys criticism, but it is sometimes necessary. If you get angry because your supervisor gives you negative feedback, get control of yourself before responding. Count to 10 if there is no other way to cool off. *Never get into a shouting match with your supervisor.*

▓ **Know what it is you have done wrong.** Your supervisor may be so upset with something you've done that you aren't sure what the problem

135

is. Apologize if you made a mistake, and ask for an explanation about exactly what you did wrong and the correct thing to do in the future.

◼ **Thank your supervisor for compliments.** You must learn to accept praise as well as criticism. Acknowledge compliments with a simple "Thank you."

◼ **Ask for feedback.** Some supervisors are not good about giving feedback. If you aren't sure what your supervisor thinks about the work you are doing, ask! Let him or her know you want to succeed on the job and you need to know how you're doing.

Key Definition

Performance Appraisal

A *performance appraisal* is a formal report about your job performance based on your supervisor's evaluation. You are rated on various areas of your job. It could be a monthly, quarterly, or annual report, depending on your organization's policy. Performance appraisals are similar to report cards in school. You usually review the appraisal form with your supervisor and have an opportunity to respond to the evaluation. Coworkers may even be asked to rate your performance. Some organizations give you a chance to rate yourself. If so, you are usually expected to explain the ratings. Be honest, but don't give yourself a rating lower than you deserve. New employees usually receive a performance appraisal at the end of their probation period.

Applying What You've Learned

Theresa has been working for Armstrong Dry-Cleaners for two months. She works behind the counter, taking customer orders. Her supervisor tells her the business is going to expand and begin cleaning leather garments. Theresa needs to fill out a special order form for leather clothing, and she is not sure she understands all of the instructions.

1. What should Theresa do at this point?

   _____

   _____

   _____

Bryan has just finished loading a truck when his supervisor comes up to him and starts yelling. He tells Bryan that a truck he loaded yesterday had several crushed boxes on it and that Bryan better get his act together if he expects to keep his job.

1. How should Bryan respond?

   _____

   _____

   _____

Meet Your Supervisor's Expectations

This section reviews some of the little things you need to know to get along with your supervisor. These are important, because *little things* to you can become *big things* to your supervisor, as they are multiplied by all the workers he or she supervises.

There are six behaviors you should practice to satisfy your supervisor's expectations:

1. **Be truthful.** Your supervisor expects you to tell the truth at all times. If you make mistakes, don't try to cover them up by lying. Lies usually are discovered, and can be grounds for dismissal. Supervisors need employees they can count on to tell the truth. Without honesty between the supervisor and workers, it's impossible for either to do a good job.

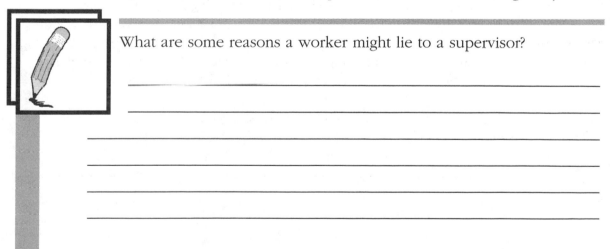

What are some reasons a worker might lie to a supervisor?

   _____

   _____

   _____

   _____

   _____

What problems could be caused for the supervisor by these lies?

_____

_____

_____

_____

_____

_____

2. **Don't extend your breaks.** Your supervisor expects you to work during your scheduled hours. Normally a full-time worker is allowed a 15-minute break mid-morning and mid-afternoon in addition to a 30- to 60-minute lunch break. When you don't return from a break on time, it can cause problems. A customer may have to wait, another worker may not be able to take his or her break, and others may not be able to finish a task until you complete your part of the job. If you can't get back from break on time, explain the reason to your supervisor. Make sure you aren't extending your breaks unless there is an exceptionally good reason.

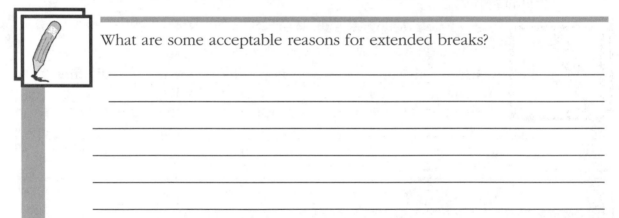

What are some acceptable reasons for extended breaks?

_____

_____

_____

_____

_____

_____

3. **Get your work done.** You should complete all assigned tasks as quickly as possible while doing the best job possible. It's difficult for a supervisor to check your work all the time. You are expected to continue working productively without a supervisor present. If circumstances prevent you from completing a job, notify your supervisor immediately. Balance your work between completing a task as quickly as possible and producing the highest quality of work you can. Ask your supervisor for feedback about how well you are meeting these priorities.

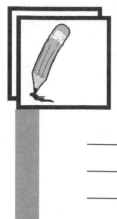

What obstacles might make it difficult or impossible for you to do your job?

_____

_____

_____

_____

_____

_____

4. **Be cooperative.** Cooperate when your supervisor asks for your help. When someone can't work at a scheduled time, be willing to change your schedule if possible. Help with a task that's not normally your responsibility. In special situations your supervisor may need more help from everybody. Cooperation is a mutual thing, and most supervisors will remember your help the next time you need a day off for a special reason. Thus, cooperation benefits you and creates a more pleasant work atmosphere.

What are some reasons for cooperation?

_____

_____

_____

_____

_____

5. **Be adaptive.** Be willing to adapt to new situations. The organization you work for needs to change as the world around it changes. Employees sometimes resist change because of poor self-esteem, threats to personal security, fear of the unknown, a lack of trust, or inability to see the larger picture.[5] When you understand the reason for resistance, you can work to reduce it. Adjustments are difficult, but your life is more pleasant when you adjust rather than trying to resist. Supervisors probably don't want to make changes any more than you do, but it is their responsibility to do so and they need your cooperation. It might help to think about the positive things that result from the changes.

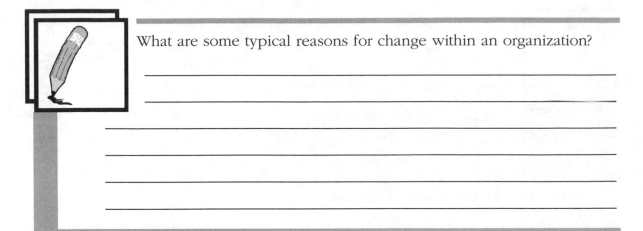

What are some typical reasons for change within an organization?

_____

_____

_____

_____

_____

6. Take the initiative. Find ways to help your supervisor. After your own work is completed, look around the work site for other tasks to do. But remember, it doesn't help anyone if your work suffers because you were trying to help with something else.

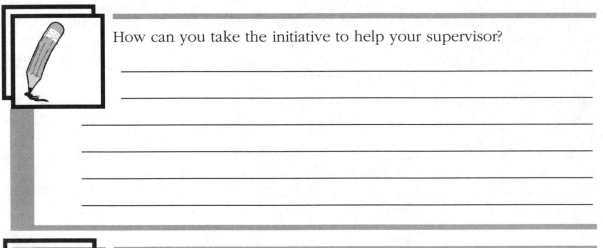

How can you take the initiative to help your supervisor?

_____

_____

_____

_____

_____

Applying What You've Learned

Tonight Jenna has a date with Brad, the quarterback at Big Moose University. Sara, her supervisor at the Bureau of Motor Vehicles, is going directly from lunch to a supervisor's meeting. Jenna knows Sara won't be back in the office until 2:30 P.M. On her lunch break, Jenna passes her favorite hairstyle salon. A quick cut would make a great impression on Brad.

1. What should Jenna do?

_____

_____

2. What could happen if she stops to get her hair cut?

_____

_____

_____

Ryan has three days off work this week. On his second day off, his supervisor calls. Ryan isn't home, but his sister takes a message. One of the other employees is sick, and the supervisor needs Ryan to work the next day. Ryan has already made plans for the day.

1. What should Ryan do?

_____

_____

_____

2. What will be the result if he goes into work? What will happen if he doesn't?

_____

_____

_____

Leslie and Tanya come into the taco shop where Brandon works just before closing time. They need a ride home. Brandon has finished nearly all of the clean-up chores, except for sweeping out the back storage room. Leslie has to be home no later than 10:30 P.M., no excuses accepted. She was grounded last week. It's 10:20 P.M. now.

1. What should Brandon do?

_____

_____

_____

2. Whose responsibility is it if Leslie gets home late?

_____

_____

_____

141

Resolving Problems

Each person looks at a situation from their own point of view. You may not always agree with your supervisor. And sometimes your supervisor will make mistakes. There may be times when you are not doing a good job. A number of situations may arise when conflicts occur. Such disagreements can be resolved by conflict resolution, through a grievance procedure, or through disciplinary procedures.

Conflict Resolution

Conflicts are a part of life. You should not try to avoid them when they arise. Talk with your supervisor about any disagreements. Below are some simple suggestions to help you keep conflicts to a minimum.

- **Don't accuse.** Everyone makes mistakes. When you make a mistake, you should do what you can to correct it. It's not a good idea to accuse your supervisor of making a mistake.

- **State your feelings.** Don't say "you" when explaining your perception of the situation. It will sound like you're accusing. Say "I feel," or "I think," or "I am" to describe your view. The supervisor does not know how you feel unless you voice your feelings.

- **Ask for feedback.** Ask your supervisor if you understand the situation correctly and have acted appropriately. It is possible you misunderstood what happened. You may find that you feel differently about the situation once it is clarified.

- **State what you want.** Know what you want done about a situation before you confront your supervisor. State your wishes clearly and respectfully.

- **Get a commitment.** After you state your feelings and what you want done, find out what your supervisor can do about the situation. Maybe no action is necessary. If no immediate action can be taken, your supervisor should commit to a date and time to let you know what will be done.

- **Compromise when necessary.** Not all problems are resolved the way you want. You may have failed to consider your supervisor's needs or the needs of the organization. How can your needs as well as your supervisor's be met? The ideal result of any conflict is that both parties are satisfied.

Most problems with your supervisor can be solved by these techniques. However, some problems can't be resolved in this manner. When such a situation occurs, you may be able to file a grievance.

Grievance Procedures

If your supervisor cannot resolve a conflict, you may resolve the problem by going through a grievance procedure. Some organizations have standard procedures, and you need to check this out. Be aware that filing a grievance almost always creates tension between you and the supervisor.

Organizations with unions usually have a procedure that has been negotiated between management and the union. If you are employed by such an organization, you will probably have a union representative with you at all steps in the grievance process. The final decision is made by an arbitrator.

Studies show that about 62 percent of nonunion companies also have formal grievance procedures.[6] Many government or government-funded organizations are required by law to have them. Some smaller organizations have no such process. You need to know your organization's procedure before filing a grievance. In nonunion organizations, you typically have no assistance filing a grievance, and the organization's personnel director or chief executive officer probably makes the final decision. Complaints of discrimination or sexual harassment often receive special attention. Such cases may require a different procedure.

You should make every attempt to resolve a conflict with your supervisor before filing a grievance. Don't tell your supervisor about the possibility of such action until you have tried every other means possible to solve the problem.

Disciplinary Action

There may be times when your work performance or behavior is unacceptable. It is your supervisor's responsibility to address the problem and to advise you on appropriate performance. If you don't correct the problem, you could face disciplinary action. Make sure you understand your employer's disciplinary process. Such procedures usually apply only to employees past their probation period. Those still on probation may be dismissed without warning. Disciplinary procedures, like grievance procedures, vary from one employer to another. The action taken will depend on the seriousness of the violation. The four steps explained below are common to many organizations.[7]

1. **Oral warning.** Your supervisor warns you that your performance is not acceptable. This applies only to less serious problems. Serious problems such as drinking or drug use probably will result in immediate suspension or dismissal. The oral warning goes into your personnel record but is removed later if no further problems arise.

2. **Written warning.** Repeated performance problems result in a written warning. This step takes place after an oral warning is issued. A written warning may become a permanent part of your personnel record.

3. **Suspension.** Suspension means you aren't allowed to work for a short period of time, sometimes three to five days. This is unpaid time. The disciplinary action becomes a permanent part of the personnel record.

4. **Dismissal.** The final step of any disciplinary process is dismissal. This means the organization won't tolerate your job performance any longer. Dismissal becomes a permanent part of the personnel record. It also means that any future employer who contacts your former employer may be told that you were dismissed from your job.

Most organizations don't want you to fail. If you are being disciplined, follow your supervisor's instructions, and you should not encounter further problems. Smaller businesses may not follow the procedure described above. You may simply get an oral warning before suspension or dismissal.

If you think you are going to be dismissed from a job, you may want to look for another job. You might also consider looking for another job when you can't resolve a problem with your supervisor.

Summing Up

Supervisors are people too. There are excellent supervisors and poor supervisors, but all supervisors appreciate good employees: They can't do their job without them. If you practice the guidelines in this chapter, you will increase the chances of establishing a positive relationship with your supervisor. If a problem does develop between you and your supervisor, try to resolve it. If a formal procedure is necessary, or your supervisor takes disciplinary action against you, make sure you understand how your organization handles such situations. Always try to abide by your employer's rules and guidelines.

Notes

1. Martin M. Broadwell, *The New Supervisor,* 4th Edition (Reading, MA: Addison-Wesley, 1990).

2. Raymond O. Loen, *Superior Supervision: The 10% Solution* (New York: Lexington Books, 1994).

3. Phillip Meilinger, "The Ten Rules of Good Followership," *Military Review* (August 1, 1994), 32.

4. Don Shula and Ken Blanchard, *Everyone's a Coach* (Grand Rapids, MI: Zondervan, 1995).

5. Barry Reece and Rhonda Brandt, *Effective Human Relations in Organizations* (Boston: Houghton-Mifflin, 1987).

6. Anne Daughtrey and Betty Ricks, *Contemporary Supervision: Managing People and Technology* (New York: McGraw-Hill, 1989).

7. Thomas Von der Embse, *Supervision: Managerial Skills for a New Era* (New York: Macmillan, 1987).

Chapter 9

Getting Along with Other Workers

Teamwork is important in any business operation. Most managers and supervisors use team-building principles. The use of the word *team* to refer to a work group is becoming increasingly common in modern organizations.[1] Teams are sometimes called quality circles, self-managing teams, self-directed work teams, or work teams. Even if your organization does not use the word *team* to refer to the work group, managers and supervisors expect you to work as part of a team. You should listen to instructions and cooperate with other employees to do the best job possible. That way everyone wins: you, the supervisor, the group, and the organization.

Get to Know Your Coworkers

The terms *team* and *work group* are interchangeable in business and are used the same way in this book. It's difficult to be a part of the team if you don't know how to get along with the other players. Getting to know your coworkers and being accepted by them helps you succeed in your job.

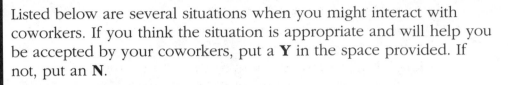

Listed below are several situations when you might interact with coworkers. If you think the situation is appropriate and will help you be accepted by your coworkers, put a **Y** in the space provided. If not, put an **N**.

____ Greet your coworkers when you arrive at work.

____ Join the office intramural sports league.

____ Ask a coworker to join you for lunch.

____ Invite your coworkers to a party at your home.

____ Tell the group how much another worker spent on a new car.

____ Bring Aunt Sally's handmade rugs to sell to your coworkers.

____ Tell the latest ethnic joke during coffee break.

____ Loan a book you enjoyed to a fellow worker.

____ Offer to take on additional duties when a coworker has to leave suddenly to tend to a sick child.

____ Repeat the latest rumor about the boss's relationship with a coworker.

____ Tell the boss when one of your coworkers leaves early.

____ Tell the group how to do the job better.

____ Tell the group how well the boss thinks you are doing.

____ Offer to give a coworker a ride to the auto repair shop.

How You Fit In

You need to know how to fit into the team. This doesn't happen immediately. It takes some time before you know how to work well with the other employees in your work group. Everyone likes to be respected for skills, knowledge, or other contributions to the group productivity, but that respect doesn't come right away. If you do your job well, your coworkers respect for you will increase over time. Meanwhile, here are a few tips to help you begin to earn respect.

■ **Know your position.** Find out what other workers expect from you in addition to your supervisor's expectations. Other workers may have a specific method they use to do a job. If you do it differently, you might upset their system. Other workers also might expect a newcomer to take over certain tasks: for instance, cleaning up after a project or at the end of the day. Go along with this. Eventually, another new worker will be hired and take over these tasks.

■ **Accept good-natured teasing.** Other workers sometimes play jokes and tease a new worker to test what kind of person he or she is. If this happens, don't get angry. Let the others know you appreciate a good joke. If this behavior doesn't cease and makes it difficult for you to do your work, you might want to talk to a coworker about it before going to your supervisor. However, if you think the jokes or teasing constitute racial or sexual harassment, let your supervisor know immediately.

■ **Do your fair share.** Everyone in a work group is expected to do his or her best. If you don't do your fair share of the work, your coworkers have to do more. After awhile, they may complain to the supervisor. The flip side is that other workers also might complain if you do too much work, because that can make them look bad. It's true that supervisors reward good workers with salary increases and promotions. But you should try to balance your work between what the supervisor expects and what your coworkers expect. When in doubt, do what the supervisor expects.

■ **Don't do other people's work.** As a member of a team, you should cooperate and help others when you are asked. However, some people try to take advantage of this cooperative spirit and push their work off on others. Remember, your supervisor will evaluate you based on how well you do *your* job. If your job suffers because you are doing someone else's work, you are likely to receive a lower evaluation. (Neither the coworker who takes advantage nor other workers will respect you for this.)

■ **Know how your team functions within the organization.** How does your team relate to other teams in the organization? What are each team's responsibilities? Remember that all teams work to accomplish the employer's goals. However, conflicts sometimes occur. Discuss these problems with all people involved. Avoid letting conflicts affect your working relationships with members of other teams. Contact your supervisor when you can't resolve conflicts with other teams. You should all be working for the best interests of the organization.

Key Definition

Synergy

Synergy describes the extra energy and capability that results in combined group efforts to accomplish an objective. It means that a team can accomplish more than the same number of people could accomplish working individually. In this case: 1 + 1 = 3.

That's why teamwork is so important to an organization. You should cooperate in every effort to develop synergy with your coworkers.

Applying What You've Learned

In the month that Rick has worked in the warehouse he has gotten to know a couple of the other workers pretty well. In fact, he went to a baseball game with Don last weekend. When he unwrapped his sandwich at lunch today, there was no meat in it. Rick turned to the other workers and yelled that he was sick and tired of their jokes, then stomped out of the lunch room, slamming the door behind him.

1. How do you think the other workers will react to Rick's outburst?

   _____

   _____

   _____

2. What should Rick have done in this situation to create a more positive relationship with other workers?

   _____

   _____

   _____

Lynette has worked at Hoover's Pharmacy for four days. Yesterday a customer broke a bottle of perfume. Mika, a worker who has worked at Hoover's slightly longer than Lynette, told Lynette to clean up the mess. Lynette cleaned up the mess. Today, a small child knocked over a display of cough medicine. Tim told Lynette to restack the boxes. Lynette got upset and told Tim to do it himself.

1. How do you think this will make the other workers feel about Lynette?

   _____

   _____

   _____

2. What do you think Lynette should have done in this situation?

   _____

   _____

   _____

The Value of Diversity

You will work with many people who are different from you. The diversity of the U.S. workforce directly affects most organizations. It's important for you to realize that differences are good. In fact, many organizations promote diversity believing it results in more productivity. Many of these organizations provide training to help people understand how to work together.[2]

On a team, the strengths of one worker can overcome the weaknesses of another. The balance created by such variety makes a team stronger. There are three basic ways that people differ from one another: in values, temperament, and individual diversity (for example, in gender, ethnicity, and age).

Values

Values are the importance we give to ideas, things, or people. The development of our values is influenced by our parents, friends, teachers, religious and political leaders, significant events in our lives, and our community. While our values may be quite different, organizational behavior expert Stephen Robbins suggests that people fall into one of three general categories.[3]

1. **Traditionalist.** People in this category value

   - Hard work
   - Doing things the way they've always been done

   - Loyalty to the organization
   - The authority of leaders

2. **Humanist.** People in this category value

- Quality of life
- Autonomy (self-direction)
- Loyalty to self
- Leaders who are attentive to worker's needs

3. **Pragmatist.** People in this category value

- Success
- Achievement
- Loyalty to career
- Leaders who reward people for hard work

Which category do you fit into? Look over the values in each of the three categories. Circle those items that you value most. Note which category has the most items circled. Then, in the space below, write the category that best describes you. Explain your reasons.

_____

_____

_____

_____

_____

_____

Effective Work Teams Blend Values

An effective work team is made up of people who have values in each category. At times the team needs the traditionalist to make sure it does what is best for the organization. At other times, the team needs the humanist, who stresses the need to balance life and work. There also are times that the team needs the pragmatist, who will strive to advance the team because it also advances personal achievement. Each person's values are important to the team.

You may not fit neatly into one category—many people don't. However, it helps us better understand and appreciate our differences with other people when we think about what category they might fall into. You can't think in terms of right or wrong, good or bad, when you talk about value differences. Each set of values is sometimes positive and sometimes negative. Appreciate the differences and learn to be tolerant of people who hold a different set.

Temperaments

Your temperament is the distinctive way you think, feel, and react to the world. Everyone has their own individual temperament. However, it's easier to understand differences in temperament by classifying people into four categories. There are many ways management specialists assess temperaments. One of the most famous is the Myers-Briggs Type Indicator. David Keirsey has adapted the Myers-Briggs and used it to identify four categories of temperament.[4] (I use Keirsey's description of the categories, but have assigned different names to each category.)

1. **Optimist.** People with this temperament

   - Must be free and not tied down
   - Are impulsive
   - Enjoy the immediate
   - Enjoy action for action's sake
   - Like working with things
   - Like to try new things
   - Can survive major setbacks
   - Are generous
   - Are cheerful

2. **Realist.** People with this temperament

   - Like to belong to groups
   - Feel obligations strongly
   - Have a strong work ethic
   - Need order
   - Are realistic
   - Find tradition important
   - Are willing to do a job when asked
   - Are serious
   - Are committed to society's standards

3. **Futurist.** People with this temperament

   - Like to control things
   - Want to be highly competent
   - Are the most self-critical of all temperaments
   - Strive for excellence
   - Judge people on their merits
   - Cause people to feel they don't measure up
   - Live for their work
   - Are highly creative
   - Tend to focus on the future

4. Idealist. People with this temperament

- Are constantly in search of their "self"
- Want to know the meaning of things
- Value integrity
- Write fluently

- Are romantics
- Have difficulty placing limits on work
- Are highly personable
- Appreciate people
- Get along well with all temperaments

What kind of temperament do you have? Go through the descriptions above and circle the items in each style that apply to you. The category in which you circle the most items is probably your temperament style.

1. Write down your temperament style.

   _____

2. Write down your secondary temperament style (second highest number of answers).

   _____

Dealing with Different Temperaments

There is no temperament style that is better than another. In fact, a team that includes people of varied temperaments is stronger. People with different temperament styles often find one another difficult to deal with because of their distinct approaches to life. When differences arise between you and a person with another temperament, follow these steps to resolve the conflict:

- Look for the positive contributions that person makes to the team.

- Identify the characteristics of your temperament that conflict with the other person's temperament.

- Talk with the person and explain what characteristics seem to cause conflict between you.

■ Ask the other person to describe which of your characteristics upsets him or her most.

■ Develop a plan of how you can work together without conflict. Often just acknowledging the differences and being willing to discuss them will reduce the conflict.

Individual Diversity

In Chapter 1, we saw that the workforce has become more diverse over the past 20 years. This trend will continue throughout the 1990s and early 2000s. There are a number of ways the workforce of tomorrow will differ from the workforce of today.[5]

■ **Gender.** By the year 2005, women will make up 47.8 percent of the workforce.

■ **Ethnicity.** Blacks and Hispanics are expected to comprise 19.5 percent of the workforce by the year 2005. Asian and other ethnic groups will make up another 3.4 percent. This means that almost a quarter of the workforce will be made up of ethnic minorities.

■ **Age.** The average age of workers will be 40.6 by the year 2005.

Individual diversity strengthens a team. Men and women often approach problems differently. Women often are more attentive to the needs of other people, while men tend to be more aggressive and ambitious.[6] Team members can learn from one another and build these positive characteristics into the work group.

People from different cultural and ethnic backgrounds look at problems from different points of view. Oriental cultures traditionally value cooperation, while Western cultures emphasize individualism. People from different cultures can help one another develop a better appreciation of their values.

A diversity of ages also can be positive. Younger workers typically bring enthusiasm and energy into a job. Older workers bring patience, maturity, and experience. These combined characteristics often make a team stronger.

No matter what the differences are, each person can contribute to the team. It's important for all members of a team to share their thoughts and ideas. Understanding one another's viewpoints will help you overcome many differences.

Basic Human Relations

Below are some practical steps you might consider as you struggle to get along with workers on your team.

1. **Get to know other workers.** Take lunch breaks with your coworkers. Join employee recreational and social activities. Listen to the things your coworkers share about their personal lives and interests.

2. **Don't try to change everything.** You're "the new kid on the block" when you start a job. Know and understand the organization before you think about changing something. Listen to others. Talk to coworkers about your ideas and get some feedback before you suggest changes.

3. **Be honest.** One of the most important things you own is a good reputation. Honesty with your coworkers will build up your reputation. It's one of the best ways to gain and keep respect.

4. **Be direct.** Let people know when they have done something that bothers you. Most people want to know when there is a problem. Don't be a complainer or a whiner: Make sure your problem is important before you discuss it with others.

5. **Avoid gossip.** Don't listen to other people gossiping about coworkers. More important, never gossip about others. When you gossip, people wonder what you say about them and often avoid you.

6. **Be positive and supportive.** Listen to the ideas of other people. When someone makes a mistake, don't criticize. It's irritating to have someone else point out a mistake. When you realize you've made a mistake, admit it and try to do better next time.

7. **Show appreciation.** Be sure you thank a coworker who does something to make your job easier. Let coworkers know you appreciate their contributions to the team. People like to be recognized and praised.

8. **Share credit when it's deserved.** Take credit for the work you do. When other coworkers assist you, make sure you credit them. People feel they have been taken advantage of if someone else takes credit for their work.

9. **Return favors.** A coworker may help you out by exchanging a day off with you. Return that favor. A sure way to make people dislike you is to only take and never give.

10. **Live in the present.** Avoid talking about the way things used to be. People don't want to hear about how great your old job was or how great former coworkers were.

11. **Ask for help and advice when you need it.** People like to feel needed. Your coworkers can be a great resource. When you aren't sure what to do, they can give you advice and assistance.

12. **Avoid battles.** Let coworkers in conflict work out their own differences. Don't take sides in their arguments. This is a sure way to develop problems with your coworkers. When you take sides, other people usually resent your interference.

13. **Follow group standards.** Every group has standards. For example, they may take a coffee break at 9:15 A.M. Stop work and go on break with them if you are able. These group standards help build a team. Most standards are not major and require little effort to follow.

14. **Take an interest in your coworker's jobs.** People like positive attention. Taking an interest in another worker's job gives that person positive attention. It also helps you better understand how your team works together.

Applying What You've Learned

Rosa's family has seven children and enjoys doing most things together. Her grandmother is celebrating her 85th birthday next Thursday, and the family has planned a surprise party for her. On Monday, when the work schedule is posted, Rosa sees she is scheduled to work Thursday evening. She is quite upset, although she knows she should have asked for the evening off before the schedule was made.

1. As a coworker, what could be your positive reaction to Rosa's problem?

   _____

   _____

   _____

2. What could be your negative reaction?

_____

_____

_____

Tyler belongs to an animal rights group. He brings literature about animal rights to work and leaves it in the break room. He refuses to eat meat because he believes killing animals for food is wrong. Tyler has invited you to join him at the next meeting of his group.

1. What could be your positive reaction to Tyler's invitation?

_____

_____

_____

2. What could be your negative reaction?

_____

_____

_____

Gwen is a very hard worker. She comes to work early and stays late. She has to be reminded to take breaks. Her main interest is her job. Sometimes, she seems to be trying to outdo her coworkers.

1. What could be your positive reaction to Gwen's work habits?

_____

_____

_____

2. What could be your negative reaction?

_____

_____

_____

Chang doesn't work on Saturdays because it's a holy day in his church, and he attends services. Last Saturday, all personnel were required to work on a special project. Chang was excused from working. Your entire work group is upset with him.

1. What could be your positive reaction to Chang's situation?

   _____

   _____

   _____

2. What could be your negative reaction?

   _____

   _____

   _____

Good Electronic Manners

Most organizations today make use of voice mail, fax machines, e-mail, and computers. This technology has resulted in a new electronic etiquette. Coworkers react to you based on your use of this technology. The following are guidelines for using technology.

1. Leave voice mail messages that are short and concise. It's frustrating to listen to long, rambling messages. Let the person know why you called, how urgent it is, and when you are available for a return call.

2. Make sure voice mail messages contain essential information. Most important are a phone number that can be used to reach you and the date and times you can be reached.

3. When you place a voice mail greeting on your phone, keep it short. Callers don't want to waste time hearing a poem or cute message, and they don't need your schedule for a week. Just let them know if your are going to be able to return their call shortly or if it will be a while.

4. Avoid leaving voice mail messages that convey anger or frustration. Otherwise, your call may not be returned. If it is returned, the person may be defensive or angry. Usually it's better to have a face-to-face discussion about a problem.

5. Avoid reading faxes sent to another person. Reading a fax is an invasion of privacy—just like opening someone's mail.[7]

6. Call someone before sending a fax, so they know it's on the way. Include a cover page so others at the receiving end know who the fax is for.

7. Many organizations have e-mail policies. Find out what these are and follow them. For example, some consider all e-mail to be company property, and any messages may be read by supervisors and managers.

8. Avoid sending e-mail messages on important matters when your message could result in a negative emotional reaction. For example, sending critical e-mail may anger the recipient much more than a direct conversation would. A personal conversation lets you observe the person's reactions. It also let's you make clear anything that could be misinterpreted.

9. Carefully consider whether other people should receive copies of a message you send to someone. A general rule is that messages containing information can be copied to other people. A message that may be considered as criticism should be kept private.

10. Avoid "flaring." This is a common occurrence with e-mail and involves sending a series of messages that become increasingly negative. For example, someone may make a suggestion and your response is negative. The person returns a negative e-mail to you. You send another e-mail that is even more negative, and the process continues until someone has the good sense to stop. When it appears that flaring is happening, talk with the person directly to avoid more conflict.

11. Don't use someone else's computer without asking. Computers may contain confidential information. Using a computer without asking may be considered a violation of privacy—just like going through a person's desk.

12. Floppy disks should also be considered personal and confidential. You shouldn't take or examine disks that don't belong to you.

Special Problems with Coworkers

Some problems require special attention. These include sexual harassment, racial harassment, dating, and violence. This section will review what you should know about each.

Sexual Harassment

Sexual harassment is unwelcome verbal or physical conduct of a sexual nature. This can include such things as these:

■ Staring at another person

■ Touching another person

■ Telling sexual jokes

■ Making sexual comments

■ Commenting on a person's sexual characteristics

■ Displaying nude pictures or obscene cartoons

Employers are required by law to protect employees from sexual harassment. You could be severely disciplined or fired for sexual harassment. The safest course is to avoid doing any of the things listed above. Even if a person doesn't object to your behavior at the time, he or she can later claim to have been intimidated. It's better to be safe than sorry.

Racial Harassment

Racial harassment is unwelcome verbal or physical actions directed at a person because of his or her race. This might include these behaviors:

■ Telling racial jokes

■ Using racial slurs

■ Commenting on a person's racial characteristics

■ Distributing racist materials

■ Excluding someone from company activities because of race

This form of harassment often results from ignorance. It's sometimes tempting to participate in the bad behavior of other workers. However, when someone engages in racial harassment, point out the harm that can result. Don't participate in any of the behaviors described.

Dating

You can get to know someone well working together, and office relationships sometimes develop into romantic relationships. No one knows how common office romances are, but dating a coworker can be risky. For one thing, romantic advances might be considered sexual harassment. In fact, repeatedly asking someone for a date after being turned down *is* considered sexual harassment.

Dating a coworker also can have a negative effect on your relationships with other workers. They may think you take advantage of your romantic relationship, that you are not doing your own work but sharing work with your romantic interest, or that you support that person's ideas or actions simply because you are dating him or her.

Another problem that can result from dating a coworker is that your attention is no longer on your job. You think about the other person instead of concentrating on your work. You may want to talk with your date rather than work, or find yourself supporting your sweetheart's actions and ideas even when you have doubts about them.

Another concern to think about is breaking up. What effect will your break-up have on your job performance and working relationship with the person? When you must work with that person everyday, you may experience a great deal of discomfort and stress.

Some organizations have a policy about dating coworkers. Be sure to find out if your employer has such a policy. If you develop a romantic interest in a coworker, be discreet. Don't talk about it in the office. Don't spend any more time with that person than is normally required. Try to separate how you behave toward the person at work and on a date.

Violence in the Workplace

You have a one in five chance of being involved in a violent act at work.[8] Violence ranges from being struck to being raped or killed. People being killed by coworkers make headlines, but fist fights are far more common. So what can you do to avoid violence?

1. People sometimes get angry. When you get angry in return, it creates the potential for violence. Tell the person that you want to solve the problem and anger won't help. Walk away from the person if necessary.

2. If a coworker threatens you with violence, notify your supervisor. You're not in school anymore, and there is no need to tolerate a bully. Coworkers who threaten violence can be fired.

3. Violence sometimes occurs because a worker has mental or emotional problems. You many notice signs of this. A person who is a "loner" and completely withdraws from other workers is exhibiting unusual behavior. This person lets stress build up and doesn't express it. Other workers may appear to always be angry and verbally or physically strike out at everyone. Still others might have mental illness such as paranoia. Talk with your supervisor when you observe strange behaviors like those described.

Not all violence can be prevented. But it can be reduced if you take steps to avoid it and alert your supervisor about potential problems.

Summing Up

Becoming part of the work team is important to your success on the job. Your relationship with other workers will affect your performance. Your contribution to the team will influence the way your supervisor appraises your job performance. Getting along with your coworkers is not difficult. It takes an understanding of yourself and an appreciation for differences between people. Finally, it takes a commonsense approach to human relations. When all else fails, treat your coworkers as you would like to be treated.

Notes

1. George Henderson, *Human Relations Issues in Management*, (Westport, CT: Quorum Books, 1996).

2. Stephen M. Paskoff, "Ending the Workplace Diversity Wars," *Training* (August 1996), 42.

3. Stephen Robbins, *Organizational Behavior: Concepts, Controversies, and Applications* (Englewood Cliffs, NJ: Prentice-Hall, 1989), 120.

4. David Keirsey and Marilyn Bates, *Please Understand Me: Character and Temperament Types,* 5th Edition (Del Mar, CA: Prometheus Nemesis Books, 1984).

5. Howard N. Fullerton, Jr., "The 2005 Labor Force: Growing, but Slowly," *Monthly Labor Review* (November 1995), 29.

6. Judith Stevens-Long, *Adult Life: Developmental Process* (Palo Alto, CA: Mayfield Publishing, 1984).

7. Sheri Roesn, "Voice Mail, 'Casual Day,' Other Developments Create New Office Etiquette Dilemmas," *Communication World* (August 1, 1995), 28.

8. Thomas Capozzoli and R. Steve McVey, *Managing Violence in the Workplace* (Delray Beach, FL: St. Lucie Press, 1996).

Chapter 10

Meeting the Customer's Expectations

You've read about the importance of getting along with coworkers and your supervisor. There is one other group of people who are very important in the workplace: the customers. Customers are important to business because they buy the products or services. This provides the income business needs to survive and make a profit. Without customers, a business will fail. Customers are important to government and nonprofit agencies because their satisfaction affects public support and continued funding. In this chapter, you'll learn about good customer service and the skills you need to provide it.

The Customer Is Always Right

Providing good customer service is important to the success of any organization. Businesses spend billions of dollars advertising and promoting products or services in an effort to get new customers. Customers who buy a product or service are satisfied primarily by three things: price, quality, and customer service. Their decision to buy now and in the future is affected by how satisfied they are with your organization's ability to fulfill these three things. Just which is the most important? According to one study, here are the primary reasons businesses loose customers.[1]

■ Died	1%
■ Moved away	3%
■ Influenced by friends	5%
■ Lured away by the competition	9%
■ Dissatisfied with product	14%
■ Turned away by an indifference on the part of an employee	68%

This study illustrates how critical customer service can be. The service you provide to customers makes a major difference in their decision to buy from a company.

What Is Good Customer Service?

Most of us experience customer service daily when we go to the grocery store, buy gas for the car, eat at a restaurant, call a business, place a catalog order, or buy clothes. Our most common activities often make us customers. Think about your experiences as a customer.

These should help you understand what good customer service means. In the following checklist, mark those items that are important in giving good customer service. Write additional items on the blank lines following the list.

❏ Smiling at customers

❏ Greeting customers

❏ Opening doors for customers

❏ Answering phone calls in a cheerful manner

❏ Letting customers on the phone talk with any employee

❏ Talking with friends while a customer waits

❏ Telling the customer that you want to solve his or her problem

❏ Asking a customer if he or she need help

❏ Letting a customer just wander around the store looking for something

❏ Listening politely to what a customer is asking

❏ Calling a customer back who has left a phone message

❏ Doing exactly what the customer requests

❏ Putting a customer on hold and letting him or her wait

❏ Not expressing anger at a customer who yells at you

❏ Telling the customer about a bad customer service experience you had at another business

Are there other things that happen to you as a customer that make you feel good about a business? If so, list them below.

❏ _____

❏ _____

❏ _____

❏ _____

❏ _____

Are there other things that happen to you as a customer that make you upset with a business? If so, list them below.

❑ _____

❑ _____

❑ _____

❑ _____

❑ _____

In one or two sentences, define good customer service.

_____

_____

_____

_____

_____

One simple definition of good customer service is treating customers the way you would like to be treated. The exercise you just completed gave you some guidelines about how this can be done. In the next section, we'll look at some specific ways to provide good customer service.

Providing Good Customer Service

Customer service begins the moment a customer contacts your business. This contact may be a visit, phone call, letter, fax, e-mail, or even a visit to the organization's web site. Your treatment of the customer affects several actions. First, it makes a difference in how the customer treats you. Second, it determines whether the customer buys the product or service sold by the business. Third, it affects what the customer thinks about your organization and whether he or she will return. The following behaviors help make customers feel good about the service they receive.

Have a Good Attitude

Customer service begins with you and your attitude. It's easy to get caught up in the busy work that makes up every job and think it's the most important thing we do. But think again. The most important thing we do is serve customers. When a customer asks for assistance, don't consider it an interruption of your work. Instead, think of it as your primary job.

Too often, workers see customers as a nuisance. You have probably seen this attitude displayed when you've been a customer. This is what frequently prompts a worker to keep talking on the phone, doing paperwork, or attending to other things while the customer waits. This attitude is sensed by a customer and starts the encounter off on the wrong foot. The next time you think of a customer as a disruption remember this: This is the person who actually pays your salary. Without customers, none of us is needed for the job.

Make the Customer Feel Good

Ken Blanchard, a leading business expert, says that if you deliver a hug along with everything else the customer expects, you can create a raving fan.[2] A hug is any gesture designed to make the customer feel better. You should go out of your way to help customers who seek service from your organization. This means being polite, courteous, and always thinking about the customer's needs.

A nice smile helps when people feel happy. When you encounter customers politely ask how you may help them. Say please and thank you. Thanking the customer for their visit or purchase is important. Holding doors open and carrying packages are all courteous actions that help customers feel good about service.

Greet Customers

It's important to make customers who come into your business feel welcome. This is most apparent at large discount and grocery stores, many of which now employ greeters to welcome shoppers. Think about times you've gone into a business only to have an employee ignore you. It doesn't make you feel positive about the business. A greeting should be polite and make the customer feel like you're interested and ready to help. For example, "Hello, may I help you?" indicates this attitude to a customer.

Whenever a customer comes into a business, immediately acknowledge his or her presence. There are some mistakes that many employees make at this point, and you should avoid them.

■ **Don't keep talking with another customer.** Balancing the needs of several customers at once can be difficult. But it's important to do this, or a customer may feel unwelcome. When a second customer comes into your work area, politely excuse yourself from the first customer. Go to the new customer and tell the person that you'll help him or her as soon as you're done with the other customer.

■ **Don't keep doing another task.** Remember, giving customer service is your first and most important task. Have you ever gone into a business and had to wait for an employee to finish a task? How did it make you feel? Most people feel like they are less important than other work the employee is doing. Put aside your task, even if it means repeating previous steps.

■ **Don't keep talking on the telephone.** The customer who came to your business took the time to travel there. You should show an appreciation for this by paying attention to his or her needs. Tell the person you're talking with on the phone that you need to call him or her back as soon as you are finished with a customer. This is particularly true if the call is personal. Even when it is another employee, it should be understood that the customer comes first. If you are talking with a customer on the phone, you might want to tell them that you have to put them on hold for just a few seconds. While the first customer is on hold, explain the situation to the new customer and say you'll be with him or her as soon as possible.

Listen to the Customer

It's important to practice good listening skills when talking with customers. The customer has all the information you need to provide topnotch service.[3] However, this doesn't mean customers can clearly express their needs. Your role is to make sure that the customer's needs are plain and understood by both parties. Here are some steps that help.

■ **Be attentive.** Assure the customer that you are listening. Often the greeting is a verbal expression of this fact. Look the person in the eye and display body language that shows you are interested. Smiling, nodding, and similar body language shows you are paying attention.

■ **Listen without interrupting**. Let the customer explain what he or she wants without interrupting. A conversation is more difficult when someone interrupts. It makes it difficult to remember your train of thought. You may have questions as the customer speaks, but wait until the person has finished talking to ask them. In fact, when you take time to listen to everything the customer has to say, many of your questions get answered.

■ **Ask questions.** Once the customer has expressed a need or placed an order, ask questions if you have them. Ask open-ended questions that can't be answered yes or no. When the customer uses a word or term that isn't familiar, ask for an explanation. Perhaps the customer has "rambled" and you aren't sure what is needed. In this case ask specific questions to help the customer to focus his or her answer. For example, you might ask, "Exactly what you are trying to do?" or "What do you want to have happen?"

■ **Repeat the need.** When you think you understand what the customer wants, repeat it back. This is one way to ensure that you both are clear about what is expected. If the customer confirms that you are correct, then you can provide the requested service. If there is still some misunderstanding, ask more questions, then repeat what you believe the customer wants. Continue this process until everyone is in agreement about what the customer wants.

■ **Negotiate the final result.** In *The Customer Is Usually Wrong!* Fred Jandt points out that it's not always possible to give the customer exactly what he or she wants.[4] When this happens, you must negotiate. The goal here is to create a win-win outcome. This means that the customer and you each get something positive out of the situation. You might be able to do this by offering an alternative to what the customer wants.

For example, say a person comes into a government employment program office and asks for assistance in preparing a resume. This isn't a service the program provides. However, there is a workshop on job-seeking techniques, and this would be a better service for the person. The workshop teaches about preparing resumes but, more important, it teaches job seekers everything they need to know about finding the job. This is really what the customer needs. The customer wins because he or she has a real need met, and you win because the program is able to serve another person.

Take Action

As soon as you know what the customer wants, you can take action to provide the service or product. This is where you can make a positive impression. Give the customer the product and service he or she wants … plus some. Meeting a customer's expectations results in a satisfied customer, but going beyond what is expected creates a satisfied and loyal customer.

How do you go beyond what customers expects? Do exactly what they request. Then do something special. For example, let's say a customer orders a diet cola. Get the cola as quickly as possible, because this action is expected. Then tell the customer that refills are free—assuming this is restaurant policy. A free-drink policy is sometimes assumed. You may know it, and regular customers may know it, but telling the customer makes him or her feel good.

Applying What You've Learned

Esther works as a nursing assistant in a hospital. One of the patients in her assigned area has just had back surgery. It is difficult for him to get out of bed without assistance. In the past hour, the patient has put on the service light three times. It always happens when Esther is busy doing something else.

1. If you were Esther, what would do to create a positive customer attitude?

   _____

   _____

   _____

2. What could Esther do to show exceptional customer service to the patient?

   _____

   _____

   _____

Janet works as an auto mechanic in an independent repair shop. One afternoon she is at the shop by herself working on an alignment job, when a customer comes in the door. She is at a point where it is difficult to stop what she is doing without having to repeat some of the work.

1. What do you think Janet should do?

   _____

   _____

   _____

2. What can she do to make the customer feel welcomed?

   _____

   _____

   _____

Iliana works for an insurance agent. A policyholder comes into the office and wants to buy insurance coverage for her new computer. The customer didn't bring the serial number for the computer with her. Iliana can't complete the necessary forms for the coverage without the serial number.

1. How do you think this situation makes the customer feel?

   _____

   _____

   _____

2. What can Iliana do to help satisfy the customer's needs?

   _____

   _____

   _____

Basic Customer Needs

Every customer has specific needs. However, all customers come to an organization with some basic needs. Karen Leland and Keith Bailey identify six basic customer needs[5]:

1. Friendliness

2. Understanding and empathy

3. Fairness

4. Control

5. Options and alternatives

6. Information

As you serve customers, keep these needs in mind. Try to meet these needs because if you do, a customer usually will be satisfied even when you can't meet a specific need. For example, let's say you go into a music store looking for a particular CD. The clerk smiles and greets you in a friendly way, finds out the CD title you want, and comments on your good taste in music. Then he helps you look for the CD, but doesn't find it. Next, he looks in the computer records and tells you that the disk has been ordered and should be in by the middle of next week. The clerk then gives you the option of reserving a copy of the CD—and makes it clear that you don't have to put any money down. He also tells you about another music store that might have the CD. When you leave the store. you don't have the CD, but chances are you feel good about the service you received because the clerk met your basic needs.

Good Customer Service on the Telephone

Most businesses serve customers over the telephone. Sometimes this is the primary way customers are served. Examples of this kind of business include carry-out restaurants, catalog dealers, and computer support hotlines. Because this is how a lot of business gets done in most companies, it's important to know how to give good customer service over the phone.

Answer the Phone Promptly

People calling on the phone expect to get an answer quickly. When the phone rings too many times, the caller often hangs up. This is one reason that many businesses have a "three-ring policy."[6] You should make an attempt to answer the phone as quickly as possible. Stop whatever else you're doing and come back to it after answering the phone. When you're talking with someone else, excuse yourself and answer the phone.

Proper Greetings

There are several points of information you should give the caller when you answer the phone. First, identify the business you work for by name. This lets customers know right away they have reached the right number. Second, identify yourself by giving your first name. It isn't important immediately to give your last name, because the caller probably won't remember both. Third, ask how you can help the caller.

There is a slight change that should be made when customers are first greeted by a receptionist or automatic answering service. In this case, customers already know they have reached the proper business. You need only give your name and ask how you might help.

Listen to the Customer

The same guidelines should be followed as for the customer who comes to your business. It is even more important to listen carefully to what the person is saying because you aren't able to observe body language. Ask questions that help you understand what the customer needs. When you are certain that you know what the customer wants, repeat the message.

Take Action

Once you have heard what the customer wants, explain exactly what you are going to do. This is important on the phone because the caller can't see what you are doing. Once the customer understands what is going to be done, you can complete the action.

175

Putting a Customer on Hold

Sometimes you must put a caller on hold while trying to satisfy a request. Being put on hold is unpleasant. Here are some steps that you can follow to make this a more pleasant experience for the caller.

1. Explain what you need to do and why it is necessary to put the person on hold.

2. Ask if it is all right to put the caller on hold.

3. Offer to call the customer back if it's going to take more than 2 or 3 minutes to satisfy the need.

4. Estimate the time it will take to complete the action. For example, you might say, "It's going to be approximately a minute before I can get back to you."

5. Sometimes it takes you longer to complete the task than you anticipated. Time waiting on the phone often seems longer than it actually is. You can reduce a customer's frustration by picking up the phone and explaining the situation.

6. Inform the customer of the action you have taken and thank him or her for waiting.

Putting a customer on hold can cause several negative outcomes. The person may get tired of waiting and hang up or get irritated and become difficult to deal with. Try to avoid putting someone on hold unless it is absolutely necessary.

Transferring a Call

Sometimes a customer needs help from someone else. In this case, you have to transfer the phone call to another employee. Like being put on hold, this can be an irritation to the customer. From the customer's point of view, you are passing the buck or don't know your job. Here are some steps to help keep the customer happy.

1. Explain why you can't satisfy the request.

2. Tell the caller the name of the person who can fulfill the request.

3. Ask the caller if he or she understands or has any questions before being transferred.

4. Make sure the employee to whom you are transferring takes the call.

5. If the employee is not available, explain that you will take a message and have the person return the call.

Taking a Message

If a customer needs to talk to another employee but that person is unavailable, you'll have to take a message. Be sure to assure the customer that the call will be returned. As you take a message. here are some steps to follow.

1. Explain that the employee isn't available *in a positive way*. For example, say that he or she is in a meeting, currently out of the office, or with another customer.

2. Tell the caller when you expect the other employee to return. This should be in a general time frame such as today, tomorrow, at the end of the week, or next week. When you expect the employee to return a call the same day, you might say the person is expected to be available before lunch, after lunch, or by the end of the workday.

3. Ask the caller if he or she would like to leave a message.

4. Ask the caller for a name, telephone number, and the reason for the call. When you aren't sure about the spelling of a name, ask.

5. Repeat the information to make sure it's correct.

6. Assure the caller that the message will be passed on and that a return call will be made.

7. Write the message in clear and readable handwriting.

8. After the caller hangs up, make sure the message is placed somewhere the employee will see it. Some organizations have message boxes for this purpose. If you have to leave a message on an employee's desk, call the employee to make sure he or she received it.

Good customer service requires that messages are received and calls are returned. Make sure you do your part by getting the message to someone else. When a message is placed on your desk from a customer, return the call as quickly as possible.

Applying What You've Learned

Burton works at a Marconi's Pizza Shop. The shop has a dining room and a delivery service. Burton answers the phone between making pizzas. It's a hectic job that allows little time for breaks.

1. What problems might Burton have in giving good customer service?

   _____

   _____

   _____

2. If you were Burton, how would you answer the phone?

   _____

   _____

   _____

Allison is a salesclerk in a dress shop. While she is waiting on a customer she hears the phone ring. She is the only employee in the shop.

1. How should Allison handle the situation?

   _____

   _____

   _____

2. What should she tell the customer when she answers the phone?

   _____

   _____

   _____

Stephen works as a clerk in a video rental store. He is checking out a customer when the phone rings. The caller asks if the store has *Casablanca* and if the video is currently in.

1. What should Stephen do with the customer he is serving?

   _____

   _____

   _____

2. How should Stephen handle the customer on the phone?

_____

_____

_____

Dealing with Difficult Customers

Sometimes you have to deal with difficult customers. The difficulty may result from the customer's complaint, anger, or rudeness. There are some simple steps you can take to help in each of these situations.

Customer Complaints

Every business has customer complaints. Sometimes customers complain because of a problem your organization created. For example, a customer may have gotten a faulty product, didn't receive an order on time, or doesn't feel the product does what it should. Sometimes the complaint is about poor service. At other times, the complaint may be the customer's fault. For example, a customer broke the product, gave the wrong address for the product to be shipped to, or didn't read a description carefully before ordering a product. Regardless of the reason, keep in mind that resolving a customer complaint will probably result in a happy and loyal customer. Here are some ideas for resolving customer complaints.

1. Listen carefully as the customer explains the problem.

2. If the customer is angry, let him or her vent the anger as long as it is kept in control and doesn't offend you or other customers.

3. Ask questions until you are sure you understand the complaint, then repeat what you understand the complaint to be.

4. Find out what will satisfy the customer. Sometimes the complaint can be satisfied with a direct action. For example, a faulty product can be replaced. Sometimes a complaint can't be resolved immediately. For example, late delivery of a product can't be undone.

5. Tell the customer exactly what you plan to do to resolve the problem. Be sure that you can follow through on everything you promise or you'll end up with a bigger complaint later on.

6. Take the action you promised and let the customer know what is going to happen. Sometimes this is clear when you simply hand over a new product. Other times it may be more involved—like reprimanding an employee who was rude.

7. Contact the customer once the action is taken and make sure he or she is now happy.

Angry Customers

Customers are sometimes angry, and there may be many reasons for the anger. Usually, the anger is the result of poor service or bad products. Sometimes anger from another event is carried over to your business. For example, a customer who has been arguing with a spouse over a purchase may come into your store angry.

1. Tell the customer you want to help correct the situation that made him or her angry.

2. Explain to the person that his or her anger is making it difficult to understand the problem.

3. Ask the customer why he or she is angry, and use the same process for clarifying a need that was explained above.

4. Describe what you can do to resolve the problem and ask the customer if the solution is satisfactory. Most of the time your solution will satisfy the customer.

5. When a customer does not respond to your attempts to resolve the anger, tell him or her that you'll get your manager to help resolve the problem.

Customer Rudeness

Rudeness may be as mild as a simple lack of courtesy or as extreme as sexual or racial harassment. Most people are rude because of ignorance. Often, when someone points out that their behavior is rude, they stop.

Sometimes people are rude because it gives them satisfaction to put down other people. You will not change their behavior by returning their rudeness or getting angry. Giving good customer service doesn't require that you tolerate customer rudeness, however. There are several things you can do to deal with a rude customer.

1. Express to the customer that his or her rude behavior makes you uneasy.

2. Tell the customer you can give better service when treated with respect.

3. Ask how you can help, and provide the best service possible.

4. Provide service without mentioning the rude behavior again if it doesn't continue.

5. If the rude behavior continues, contact your supervisor and ask for assistance.

Applying What You've Learned

Abby works at a dry-cleaning business. A man comes in with a pile of shirts and says they weren't properly starched and packaged. Abby looks at the shirts and doesn't see any problem.

1. How should Abby deal with this complaint?

    _____

    _____

    _____

2. What can be done to keep this customer coming back to do more business?

    _____

    _____

    _____

Roscoe works in the produce department of a grocery store. A customer comes up to him and complains about not being able to find the apples that were in the sales ad. When Roscoe looks for the apples he can't find them either.

1. How do you think the customer will feel when Roscoe says he can't find the apples?

_____

_____

_____

2. What should Roscoe do to satisfy the customer?

_____

_____

_____

Marlene works in a childcare center. A mother comes into the room early one morning and begins yelling that her son's teddy bear hadn't been sent home with him yesterday. The children in the room are becoming upset.

1. What can Marlene do to immediately help calm the situation?

_____

_____

_____

2. What can Marlene do to help resolve the mother's anger?

_____

_____

_____

Summing Up

Customer service is important because customers are vital to business. Knowing that the customer is the most important person in the organization is the key to success. Employees must make customer service their number one job. Meeting customer needs can be accomplished by following some simple but critical steps. Keep in mind the fact that customers don't interrupt your work—they are your work.

Notes

1. Betsy Sanders, *Fabled Service: Ordinary Acts, Extraordinary Outcomes* (San Diego, CA: Pfeiffer, 1995).

2. Kenneth Blanchard and Sheldon Bowles, *Raving Fans* (New York: Morrow, 1993).

3. Robert Spector and Patrick D. McCarthy, *The Nordstrom Way: The Inside Story of America's #1 Customer Service Company* (New York: Wiley, 1995).

4. Fred Jandt, *The Customer Is Usually Wrong!* (Indianapolis: Park Avenue, 1995).

5. Karen Leland and Keith Bailey, *Customer Service for Dummies* (Foster City, CA: IDG, 1995).

6. Kristin Anderson, *Great Customer Service on the Telephone* (New York: American Management Association, 1992).

Chapter 11

Problem-Solving Skills

Managing an organization today is a complicated business. Competition from other countries is increasing, technology continues to grow more complex, government regulations are sometimes difficult to understand and follow. Faced with these complexities, employers are looking for workers who are problem solvers.

Problem solving is a highly marketable skill. Employers need people who can think on their feet. Learning to solve problems is important to your success on the job. In this chapter you'll practice seven steps to improving your problem-solving skills.

Management Through Team Work

Managers in today's business world are relying on employees and work teams to help solve many problems. This is called *employee involvement*. Teams may be expected to solve any problems that occur. For example, if the data your team enters into a computer has a lot of mistakes, the team will be asked to solve the problem. There are several reasons for the growth of employee involvement, including these:

- **Reduction of management.** In the last several years, businesses have made drastic cuts in the number of managers and supervisors they employ, thus saving a great deal of money. This means employees must assume some of the responsibilities previously performed by managers.

- **Complexity.** Worldwide competition, high technology, government regulations, and a diverse workforce all make businesses more complex. An organization needs help from every employee to solve problems in these complex areas.

- **Motivation.** Employees are motivated to do a better job when they are involved in solving problems related to their work.

- **Proximity.** Employees are closer to most problems than managers and supervisors. They often see solutions that escape managers.

- **Change.** Modern organizations go through a great deal of change. If employers want their employees to be willing to change, they must involve them in problem-solving and decision-making processes.

Key Definition

Total Quality Management Teams

Experience has shown that the most effective way to manage workers is to involve them in the problem-solving process. Employees are more motivated when they have more control over their work. Participation in problem solving gives employees that control. Employee involvement is implemented through work teams or quality circles. A *quality circle* is a group of employees who meet to identify problems and find solutions.

Sometimes the term used is *process action team*. This is a group brought together from different parts of an organization to solve problems using statistical analysis.[1] Whatever the term used, more organizations are using teams for problem solving. Their purpose is to improve the quality of services, products, and jobs.

Employees who develop good problem-solving skills become valuable members of the team.[2] They are seen as good workers who should be rewarded with promotions and raises. This section examines skills you need to become a good problem solver.

Problem Solving

In order to be logical, problem solving must be a systematic process.[3] Here are some basic assumptions for good problem solving:

- **Problems can be solved.** It's important to believe a problem can be solved. This belief motivated some of the greatest problem solvers of history, such as Thomas Edison, inventor of the light bulb; Henry Ford, the creator of modern manufacturing processes; and Jonas Salk, who discovered the polio vaccine. These people persisted despite many failures. Thomas Edison failed more than 900 times before he produced a light bulb that worked.

- **There is a cause for everything that happens.** Problems have causes. You must look for the causes to solve the problem. Often, it is only possible to find probable causes.

- **Problem solving is a continuous process.** Any problem-solving system must be a continuous process. In other words, after finishing the last step in the process, we must return to the first step and begin the process again. This gives us the opportunity to evaluate whether the solution is working or if it can be improved.

The Problem-Solving Process

The problem-solving process can develop in a number of ways, but the steps and order you follow are important. Leaving out any of the steps or doing them in a different order will limit your problem-solving abilities.

Step 1. Identify the problem. The biggest mistake you can make in solving a problem is to work on the wrong problem. Take time to discover what the real problem is. Here is an example of the importance of this step. A book store manager notices that the store is frequently out of certain titles. She defines the problem this way: "Employees need to order books when they see that we have run out of a title." She then begins to work on getting employees to reorder books. However, the real problem could be something else. It could be that a standard number of books is ordered for each title when larger quantities should be ordered for more popular books. In this case, the problem should be defined as "how to improve inventory control."

Step 2. Gather and organize data about the problem. You should gather as much data on the problem as possible. The best way to collect data is to observe what happens. Other good methods include talking with people involved and reading reports. Organize the data in a way that will help you arrive at a solution. This process is called *analysis*. Analysis requires some mathematical skills. There are three simple methods you can use to analyze data: frequency tables, percentages, and graphs.

Step 3. Develop solutions to the problem. After collecting data about the problem, you can begin to develop solutions. Develop as many solutions as possible. There are several things you can do to develop solutions.

- **Talk to other people.** Talk the problem over with coworkers who have experienced the problem and find out how they solved it in the past. One of the best ways to learn about something is to ask questions.[4] Ask friends from other organizations if they have had a similar problem and how they solved it. (When talking to people outside your organization, do not reveal information that would be considered confidential.)

- **Hold a group discussion.** The two most popular types of group discussion are as follows:

  1. **Brainstorming.** Brainstorming sessions involve a group of workers trying to come up with as many ideas as possible. There are some important rules to follow when brainstorming. First, don't criticize any ideas. You want to develop as many ideas as possible without being concerned about their quality. Second, stretch for ideas. When the group thinks it has exhausted all ideas, try again. Third, write all ideas on flip charts so that the entire group can see what's been suggested.

  2. **Nominal group technique.** This is a more controlled method than brainstorming. First, each person thinks of as many ideas as possible and writes them on a piece of paper. Second, the group shares these ideas, taking one idea from one person at a time in a round-robin manner. Third, the group discusses the ideas. Fourth, the group ranks or rates the ideas from best to worst.

- **Change places with other employees**.[5] Spend four to eight hours in another department. See how other employees handle problems similar to ones in your department. A change in roles often provides a new viewpoint that can help you solve a problem. This method also allows employees in another department to ask you for ideas about their problems.

■ **Visit other organizations with similar problems.** You can learn a lot by discovering how other organizations solve their problems. Many businesses are willing to let you visit if you don't work for a direct competitor. Look at their solutions and evaluate how they solved similar problems. Discover how well they think the solutions work. Decide if the solutions could be used in your organization.

■ **Read about the problem.** Trade journals provide valuable information about how organizations like yours have solved problems. There are trade journals for computer dealers, retailers, publishers, fast-food restaurateurs, the list goes on and on. Since trade journals deal with businesses just like yours, they publish articles that give helpful ideas about problems. Other business magazines or books also may give you some good ideas.

Step 4. Evaluate possible solutions. There are a number of questions you should ask when evaluating possible solutions:

■ **Is the idea logical?** Look for a direct relationship between the problem and the solution. For example, giving dissatisfied customers a discount doesn't solve a poor customer service problem.

■ **How much will it cost?** You may have a great idea, but if it isn't affordable, it doesn't do the organization any good. Some problems are not complicated, so the solutions are not costly. However, costs for solutions to more complex problems can vary greatly. For example, pizza delivery time might improve if a store bought a new truck, but it may not be able to afford one.

■ **Does the organization have workers who know how to implement the solution?** Some solutions require specialized knowledge. Without employees who have that knowledge, the solution won't work.

■ **Is the solution timely?** Some problems need immediate solutions. Some ideas are good, but take too long to implement. Sometimes you must choose two solutions: one that works immediately and another that will be a better solution for the future. For example, a new printing press will improve the quality of the company's printed documents, but delivery is three months away. The immediate solution might be to reduce press speed, re-ink more often, and have employees work overtime.

Even after applying these rules, it's difficult to select the right solution from a large number of ideas. Two ways to help sort ideas are rating and ranking.

- **Rating** is a process in which each idea is evaluated separately. You apply all four questions above to each idea. Then you rate it on a scale of 1 to 5, 1 being a great idea and 5 a terrible idea. One drawback to this method is that you may end up with several ideas that are rated equal or almost equal.

- **Ranking** involves looking at all ideas, choosing the best, and ranking it number one. Then you compare the remaining ideas and select number two. Continue this process until all ideas have been ranked. A weakness of this method is that it's difficult to rank more than 10 ideas at a time.

Probably the best way to select the number one idea is to use both rating and ranking. First, rate all ideas. Then rank the top 10. This uses the strengths of each method and omits their weaknesses.

Step 5. Select the best solution. By the time you complete the analysis, you should be able to decide on the best solution. The best solution may not always be the top idea, but it will usually be among the top three to five ideas. Keep these three things in mind when choosing a solution:

- **The best idea may not be affordable.** This means you should select an idea that will solve the problem without greatly increasing cost. If the top two or three ideas are basically equal, select the less costly one.

- **There's always risk involved.** No solution will be foolproof. This often keeps people from making a decision. You can try to reduce the risk, but you can't eliminate it.

- **Don't worry about being wrong.** Mistakes can't be totally eliminated. Think about what to do if the solution fails. Planning ahead for errors means they can be corrected more quickly.

Step 6. Implement the solution. A good idea can be ruined if you fail to implement it correctly. Here are some guidelines for implementing ideas.

- **Believe in the idea.** Never implement an idea you don't think solves a problem. Sometimes, if people believe an idea will be successful, it's easier to overcome difficulties that would otherwise jeopardize it.

- **Convince others to support the idea.** When a group solves the problem, you already have this step covered. It's critical to get the supervisor's support for any idea. A group solution helps convince your supervisor to support a solution. However, if you develop a solution by yourself, you need to sell it to other people.

- **Don't let fear hold you back.** It's normal to be afraid of failure. Worries about losing your job or reputation if an idea fails need to be kept in check. People sometimes wait too long before implementing a solution. Remember, inaction can kill a good idea.

- **Follow through.** A solution shouldn't be immediately rejected because it doesn't work. It takes time for ideas to work. Continue trying the solution until you know why it isn't working before taking a new approach.

Step 7. Evaluate the solution. Within a reasonable period of time, evaluate the effectiveness of the solution and decide if it's working. One good way to evaluate is to repeat the analysis step (Step 2). For example, go back and do another frequency table to find out if customers are happier or if production or quality is improved.

Creative Thinking

Many organizations realize they must be innovative to compete with other businesses.[6] So employers want workers who think creatively. Creativity is the ability to think of new ideas. This may mean applying old ideas to new problems or coming up with entirely new ideas. Here are some suggestions to help you think creatively.

1. **Don't let the problem limit your thinking.** Our thinking process sometimes limits the way we look at a problem. The following exercise illustrates blocks to creative thinking.

Exercise 1. Connect all nine dots with four straight lines without lifting your pencil off the paper. (Look at the end of the chapter for the solution to this problem.)

2. **Look at the problem from different viewpoints.** Here's a simple way to do this. List ridiculous solutions to the problem. Then turn those ideas around and ask how they might make sense. This process is illustrated in the following example.

Your supervisor has asked you and the other employees how to increase the number of customers who visit the shoe store where you work. Here some ideas:

■ Give shoes away

■ Yell at people to come into the store

■ Carry every style of shoe made

■ Pay customers to take shoes

Making these ideas workable would give you the following:

■ Discount shoes as much as possible

■ Get people's attention through advertising

■ Have a wide variety of styles

■ Include a free pair of socks with each purchase

3. **Use hazy thinking.** Other words for hazy are unclear or vague. Sometimes we're very specific and take things too literally in the problem-solving process. Maybe our thinking should be hazy and unclear. The next exercise illustrates how literal thinking can block creativity.

Exercise 2. Look at the letters below. Eliminate five letters to find one familiar word in the English language. After you've tried solving the problem, look at the answer at the end of this chapter. This exercise shows that thinking in such specific ways blinds us to alternative ideas.

> F H I E V L E I L C E O T P T T E E R R S

4. **Joke about the problem.** Humor is a good way to find the alternative solutions to a problem. Humor often relies on expectations. You are led to think one way, then surprised after seeing another way. This old riddle is an example. *Question:* What is black and white and read all over? *Answer:* A newspaper. When this joke is spoken, "read" is usually interpreted as "red," because black and white lead a person to think about colors. Humor might allow you to view the problem in an entirely different way—an unexpected way.

5. **Give yourself time to think.** Take time to think about the problem and solutions. Relax and look at the ideas you've come up with.[7] Don't allow anything to distract you. Get away from phones, customers, coworkers, radios, televisions, and anything else that might distract you. Write down your thoughts during this time or, better yet, record them on tape so you're not distracted by writing. Then get away from the problem. Do something entertaining. Get together with friends. Relax. Often, this relaxation frees your subconscious to come up with more possible solutions.

There are other methods for being creative, such as brainstorming and researching a problem. There are many excellent books on creative thinking. Find one and learn more about this valuable skill.

Summing Up

Problem solving is an important skill for employees in modern business. Many organizations expect every worker to contribute solutions to problems. You should practice your problem-solving skills whenever you get the chance. These skills will improve as you apply the techniques in this chapter.

Solutions to Creative Exercises

Exercise 1: Most people see that the dots make a square. So they think they can't make their lines go outside this box. However, the instructions don't place this limit. You can't solve the problem unless you go outside the lines.

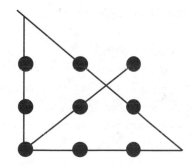

Exercise 2: You were to cross out five letters to find one familiar word. Most people will try to follow this instruction by crossing out five letters. However, the way to solve the problem is to cross out the words *five letters*:

F̶H̶I̶E̶V̶L̶E̶I̶L̶C̶E̶O̶F̶P̶T̶T̶E̶E̶R̶R̶S̶

Notes

1. Bob Bookman, "Energizing TQM With Right-Brain Thinking," *Training* (August 1992), 62.

2. Dennis Potthoff, Catherine Yeotis, Mary Butel, Tim Smith, and Janet Williams, "Responding to Industry's Call: Using Discrepant Events to Promote Team Problem-Solving Skills," *Clearing House* (January 1, 1996), 180.

3. Alfred Travers, *Supervision: Techniques and New Dimensions* (Englewood Cliffs, NJ: Prentice-Hall, 1988).

4. Ronald Gross, *Peak Learning* (New York: Putnam, 1991).

5. Michael Michalko, "Bright Ideas," *Training and Development* (July 1994), 44.

6. William Miller, *The Creative Edge: Fostering Innovation Where You Work* (Reading, MA: Addison-Wesley, 1987).

7. James Adams, *The Care and Feeding of Ideas* (Reading, MA: Addison-Wesley, 1986), 123-124.

Chapter 12

Do the
Right Thing

Ethics are principles or standards that govern our behavior. Ethical principles usually are set by society. Our communities, organizations, religions, and families establish ethical principles that guide us in our daily actions. In this chapter, we'll examine ethical behavior on the job. This is what governs the way you behave toward your employer, supervisor, coworkers, and customers. As we begin, let's look at how you view ethical behavior.

1. List below the reasons you feel ethical behavior is important.

    _____

    _____

    _____

2. List common ethical principles or ideals observed by most people.

    _____

    _____

    _____

3. Now list some job situations in which you would need to apply ethical principles.

    _____

    _____

    _____

Ethical Problems for Business

There are many reasons businesses are concerned about the ethical behavior of employees.

■ Employee theft costs U.S. businesses more than $60 billion each year.[1] In fact, 50 percent of all working students admit stealing from companies, and almost 35 percent said they steal $10 or more a month.[2]

■ Employees who copy software illegally can cause an employer to be sued. Violation of copyright laws can result in fines of up to $100,000 and five years imprisonment for each illegal use. Moreover, the Software Publisher's Association targets smaller companies.[3] It's clear that an employee making illegal copies of software costs an employer.

■ Employees who use drugs on the job are 3.6 times more likely to have an accident.[4] Higher accident rates cost an employer more money in worker compensation insurance payments and loss of productivity and, more importantly, hurt people.

Unethical behavior is costly to business and causes morale problems. Employees who behave unethically are almost always fired. In addition, the employee's reputation is hurt. Most people feel guilty about unethical behavior—even if they are punished. In this chapter, you'll learn what behavior is ethical and what is unethical. You'll also discover some basic principles that can guide you in making ethical decisions.

What Is Ethical Behavior?

At first glance, ethical behavior seems easy. All you've got to do is "the right thing." Knowing what the right thing is for every situation is the hard part. Also, what you consider "right" or "ethical" may differ from what others consider them. Most people learn ethical behavior while growing up and use the same principles as adults.

Ethical Decision-Making Problems

Sometimes it's hard to know what is the right behavior. There are three basic problems most people have when trying to decide the right thing to do.

1. **Not knowing what is expected.** There may be times you face a situation and don't know what is right or wrong.

   ■ For example, you deliver a package and the customer offers you a tip. You're a new employee and don't know if the company allows you to accept tips. You also don't know if you're supposed to report any tips.

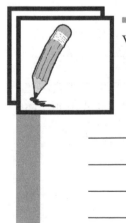

What would you do in this situation?

_____

_____

_____

_____

_____

_____

2. **Conflicts in ethical standards.** A major problem can result when your ethical standards conflict with those of others. This kind of conflict can occur between you and your coworkers, supervisor, or the organization itself.

■ For example, you and two other workers are out on a repair job for a telephone company. The other workers decide to report that the job will take three hours, when in fact it will take only two hours. They plan to spend the extra hour drinking in a bar.

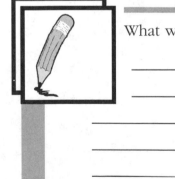

What would you do in this situation?

_____

_____

_____

_____

_____

■ You may have ethics conflicts with your supervisor. For example, you work for a painting contractor. At the end of a day's work, your supervisor tells you to take some partially empty paint, varnish, and turpentine cans to the county landfill. You know it's illegal to dispose of these materials in a landfill.

What would you do?

_____

_____

_____

_____

_____

■ Your ethics may conflict with those of the organization. This can happen when a company supports policies you believe are wrong. For example, you work for a restaurant that regularly substitutes a lower grade of meat than is advertised on the menu.

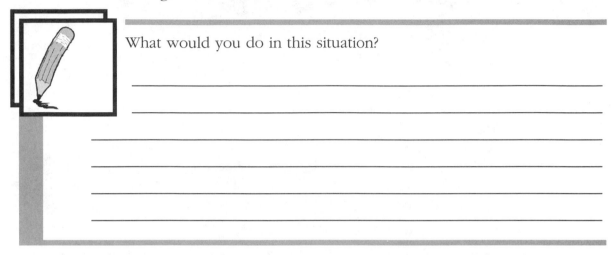

What would you do in this situation?

_____

_____

_____

_____

_____

_____

3. **Dilemmas about a situation.** Not every ethical decision is strictly right or wrong. In these situations it can be very difficult to decide how to behave.

■ For instance, you are a bank teller. A coworker confides that he is working on a GED. You know that a high school diploma or GED is one of the bank's hiring requirements. It's obvious the coworker lied on his application. In the entire time you have known him, he has always done an excellent job as a teller. You know that he has a wife and two children who depend on his income from this job.

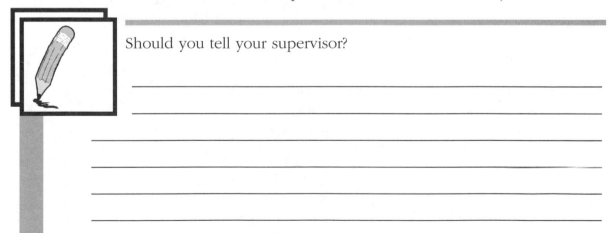

Should you tell your supervisor?

_____

_____

_____

_____

_____

_____

Guidelines for Making Ethical Decisions

The problems illustrated above show the difficulty in making ethical decisions. Did you have trouble trying to decide how you would act in the situations? Most people would have some difficulty. However, there are some questions you can ask yourself when making these decisions. These questions can help guide your behavior. You may need to answer several or all of the questions before you can make the right decision. Just because you can answer one question doesn't mean the act you are considering is ethical.

1. **Is it legal?** This refers to local, state, and federal laws. Laws express the ethical behavior expected of everyone in society. You should consider if you could be arrested, convicted, or punished for your behavior.[5] In the example of disposing paint cans in a landfill, it's clear that doing what the supervisor wants is illegal. When you do something illegal, your behavior will not be excused simply because you were ordered to do it.

2. **How will it make you feel about yourself?** A good self-concept is one key to doing the right thing. A book by Norman Vincent Peale and Ken Blanchard states, "people who have a healthy amount of self-esteem tend to have the strength to do what they know is right—even when there are strong pressures to do otherwise."[6] What you're really asking is this: *Am I at my best?* Most of us want to do our very best. We want to look at ourselves in the mirror without feeling guilt.

3. **How do others feel about it?** You should discuss ethical problems with others. It may be difficult to share the problem with your supervisor. Talk with a coworker you trust. You can talk to friends, relatives, religious leaders, or anyone whose opinion you respect. Don't just talk to people you think will agree with you.[7] Listen to advice from others, but don't assume that the majority is always right.

4. **How would you feel if the whole world knew about it?** Take the *60 Minutes* test. What if a reporter from *60 Minutes* showed up to broadcast what you are doing? If you don't want coworkers, supervisors, friends, relatives, or the community to know what you are going to do, *don't do it.*

5. **Does the behavior make sense?** Is it obvious that someone could be harmed? Might you harm someone physically, mentally, or financially? Is it obvious that you will get caught? This last question shouldn't be the only thing you consider, but you should keep it in mind.

6. **Is the situation fair to everyone involved?** Ethical behavior should ensure that everyone's best interests are protected.[8] Look at how everyone can benefit, but realize that everyone will not benefit equally by the decision you make. No one should receive a great gain at the expense of someone else.

7. **Will the people in authority at your organization approve?** How does your supervisor feel about the behavior? What would the manager of your department say? Would it be approved by the organization's lawyer? Find out what those in authority think about the situation. This doesn't guarantee the right decision. Sometimes people in authority support unethical behavior. You aren't necessarily relieved of responsibility because a supervisor approves a certain act.[9] However, asking for approval indicates what behavior is thought to be right by people in authority at your organization.

8. **How would you feel if someone did the same thing to you?** This is the *Golden Rule,* or "do to others what you would want them to do to you." When applying this principle, you should look at the situation from another person's point of view. Another way to view this issue was voiced by philosopher Immanuel Kant, who suggested that what individuals believe is right for themselves they should believe is right for all others.[10] When you make an ethical decision, you should be willing for everyone else to do the same thing that you do. Avoid doing things you think would be unfair to you, because they're probably unfair to someone else as well.

9. **Will something bad happen if you don't make a decision?** There may be times when you decide to do nothing and it won't affect anyone. You may have good reasons for not wanting to get involved. However, you may be aware of a situation that could result in someone being hurt. Not taking action when you think you should can result in a major problem.

Ask as many of these questions as you can when you are trying to make an ethical decision. Asking only one is not likely to result in the best ethical choice. The more principles you can apply, the better your ethical choice will be.

Applying What You've Learned

Roger works for the license branch. Recently, he saw one of the driving examiners take a bribe from an elderly woman. Roger knows the woman. She lives alone and needs to drive her car to get groceries and do other business. He has never seen the examiner take a bribe before.

1. What do you think Roger should do?

_____

_____

_____

2. Explain your answer.

_____

_____

_____

Lisa works for a screw and bolt manufacturer. The company has a contract with the Air Force. Lisa knows that the bolts being made for the Air Force do not meet the required standards. She talked with her supervisor, and he said not to worry about it. He said it was up to management to correct the problem.

1. If you were Lisa, what would you do?

_____

_____

_____

2. Explain your answer.

_____

_____

_____

Jane works in a jewelry store. A customer left two rings for cleaning, but Jane accidentally gave her a receipt for just one ring. The customer didn't notice the mistake and left the store before Jane realized what she had done. One of the rings is quite beautiful. Jane thought about how nice it would look on her. She began to think about keeping the ring for herself and telling the manager the customer left only one ring. After all, the customer is very wealthy and can afford the loss.

1. What do you think Jane should do?

   _____

   _____

   _____

2. Explain your answer.

   _____

   _____

   _____

Now go back to the situations presented earlier in the chapter. Apply the ethical questions to them. What, if anything, would you do differently? Explain your reasons for each situation.

1. Taking a tip from a customer.

   _____

   _____

   _____

   _____

2. Taking an extra hour with the repair crew.

   _____

   _____

   _____

   _____

3. Dumping paint cans in the landfill.

   _____

   _____

   _____

   _____

4. Substituting lower grade meat.

_____

_____

_____

_____

5. Reporting a worker who lied on his application.

_____

_____

_____

_____

Common Ethical Problems

There are some common ethical problems workers often face on the job. Listed below are seven areas where knowing how to behave can keep a new worker out of trouble.

1. **Favoring friends or relatives.** This is a particular problem in a business that deals directly with the public. Many businesses allow employee discounts for immediate family members (father, mother, spouse, brothers, and sisters). However, friends may expect special deals and service. As a result, paying customers do not get proper service because of the attention shown to friends. Know what your employer permits and expects in these situations.

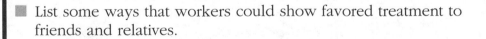

List some ways that workers could show favored treatment to friends and relatives.

_____

_____

_____

2. **Cheating the employer out of time.** An employer pays employees for time spent at work. Some workers cheat the employer out of this time in a number of ways, including these:

■ Breaking for longer periods than is allowed

■ Talking excessively with friends and relatives while at work

■ Coming to work late or leaving early

■ Hiding someplace to avoid working

■ Conducting personal business using office equipment

This kind of behavior is irritating to supervisors. Less work gets done and customers may not be satisfied. When employees behave this way, disciplinary action may be taken.

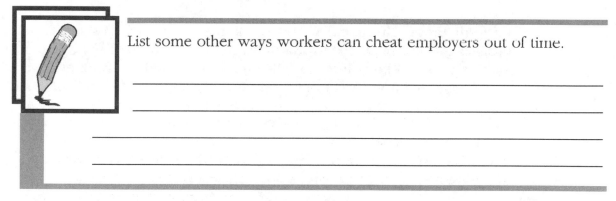

List some other ways workers can cheat employers out of time.

_____

_____

_____

_____

3. **Stealing from the company.** Taking money from the cash register or taking merchandise from a store are obvious ways of stealing. However, there are four things workers often steal without thinking of it as theft.

■ **Supplies.** People often take pens, pencils, paper, paper clips, and other supplies from their employer. It doesn't seem like a big thing because the organization has so many supplies. However, multiplied by all employees it can cost an organization a great deal of money.

■ **Photo copies.** Many employees use the copy machine for personal use without thinking of it as theft. However, it usually costs a business 2 to 5 cents per copy. Making 20 copies may cost $1. If every employee in an organization with 1,000 employees did this once a week, it would cost the employer almost $52,000 a year. Small thefts by workers can add up to major expenses for an organization.

Key Definition

Software Piracy

Copying software illegally is called *piracy*. Software is protected by copyright laws, just like books and videos. Sometimes software is made available as freeware or shareware. *Freeware* means that the program developer allows anyone to freely make copies. *Shareware* means you can use the software and make copies for others. However, you are expected to pay the program developer if you continue to use the program. Commercial software is purchased, and the right to make copies is restricted.

There are three basic rules to consider in order to avoid pirating commercial software. First, you can only install the program on one computer. Second, you can make only one copy. This copy must be stored and only used if the original is damaged. Third, you should never make copies for anyone else. A much more serious violation is to make a pirated copy and sell it.

■ **Long-distance phone calls.** This is one of the most expensive crimes in business. Telephone companies charge more during business hours. Making personal long-distance calls on the organization's phone system can add up to lots of money.

■ **Software piracy.** Computers makes it easy to copy software programs owned by an organization. This is known as piracy. It's estimated that over $15 billion in software was pirated in 1995.[11] Some organizations fire employees caught pirating software.

■ What are other ways employees steal from their employers?

_____

_____

_____

_____

4. **Abusing drugs and alcohol.** Drinking alcoholic beverages or using drugs on the job is wrong. Taking recreational drugs or nonprescription drugs is against the law. Using them on the job can result in immediate termination. There are three major job problems related to substance abuse:

■ **Lower productivity.** Employees produce fewer goods or services.

■ **Lower quality.** It's impossible to perform at your best when you are under the influence of alcohol or illegal drugs. Your quality of work will be less than your employer is paying you to provide.

■ **Safety hazards.** Substance abuse can cause many safety problems. Since reactions are slowed, workers are more likely to suffer serious or fatal injuries.

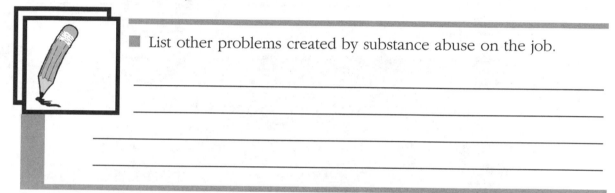

■ List other problems created by substance abuse on the job.

_____

_____

_____

_____

5. **Violating matters of confidentiality.** Some employees have access to a great deal of information. If you are in a position to handle such information, don't talk to anyone about it. This includes other workers. Confidential information may include the following:

■ **Company information.** Confidential information about a company can cause great harm if it is shared. Trade secrets about products or services can be used by competitors to duplicate products. Financial data can be used by competitors to identify weaknesses and strengths of a business. Customer lists can be used to lure customers away. These and other pieces of information should only be shared with approved people.

■ **Customers.** This could include private information, such as salary, credit history, or employment history. Less critical information like the amount of money spent with your organization, address, and telephone number could still cause harm to someone.

■ **Employees.** This may include salary, personnel records, performance appraisals, or attendance records. Talking about any of this with others could harm the employee's reputation or bring about other problems.

Many companies have policies about confidentiality. You should know your employer's policies. However, it's in everyone's best interest for you to keep all information confidential.

■ List other information that should be treated as confidential.

_____

_____

_____

_____

6. **Knowing about other employees' unethical behaviors.** One of the most difficult situations to face is knowing that another employee has done something wrong. There are two reliable ways of finding out about this type of situation:

■ The other employee may tell you personally.

■ You see the employee do something wrong. If this happens, you should feel some obligation to report the problem to your supervisor.

Gossip is another way of finding out about another employee's misdeeds. You probably should not feel obligated to report what gossip you hear to a supervisor. In fact, when you don't have firsthand information about a situation, it's usually best not to repeat what you've heard to anyone.

■ List some things you may discover about other workers that you might need to report to your supervisor.

_____

_____

_____

_____

7. **Violating the organization's policies.** Many organizations have a set of personnel policies to govern employee behavior. Policies are communicated through a policy manual or in the form of memos. As an employee, you are expected to follow these policies. You can be disciplined for violating them. It's important to know what the policies are and to follow them. Even if other workers get away with breaking the policies, you should not accept this as a good reason for breaking them yourself.

■ List some common personnel policies an organization might establish.

_____

_____

_____

_____

How you deal with ethical problems determines how successful you will be on your job. The wrong behavior could cause your supervisor to be dissatisfied with your performance and could, in fact, cause you to be fired from your job.

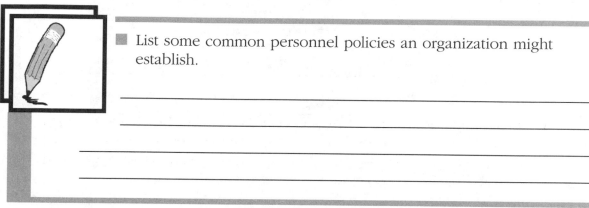

Applying What You've Learned

Shane works in the payroll department. He has several friends in the computer department. One of these friends, Fran, told him that she just got a raise. Her supervisor told her she is now the most highly paid programmer in the company. Shane knows there are several other programmers who have higher salaries than Fran has been promised. The supervisor has obviously lied to Fran.

1. Should Shane tell Fran what he knows?

_____

_____

_____

2. Explain your answer.

_____

_____

_____

Justine works in a donut shop. Some of her friends stop by late at night. She spends a lot of time talking with them, but there aren't any customers in the shop. A customer comes in and Justine immediately asks if she can help him. She then returns to her friends' table and starts talking with them.

1. Do you think Justine is doing the right thing by spending so much time talking with her friends?

_____

_____

_____

2. Explain your answer.

_____

_____

_____

Lance works at a fast-food restaurant. His family is very poor. The restaurant has a policy of throwing out hot sandwiches that aren't sold within 15 minutes. The policy also states that employees are not to take any of the sandwiches for themselves. Lance's supervisor tells him to throw away 10 cheeseburgers. He thinks about how much his family could use the sandwiches. Instead of throwing them in the dumpster, he hides them in the back of the store and takes them home when he leaves work.

1. Should Lance have done this?

_____

_____

_____

2. Explain your answer.

_____

_____

_____

Demos is a project coordinator for a state health agency. The agency just upgraded word processing programs on everyone's computer. Demos has the disks from the older version of the program. The agency will no longer use these disks, so he decides to take them home and install that software on his personal computer.

1. Is Demos doing the right thing?

    _____

    _____

    _____

2. Explain the reasons for your answer.

    _____

    _____

    _____

Summing Up

Supervisors evaluate workers based on their behavior. If they see workers doing something they consider unethical, those workers will be disciplined. To maintain a good self-concept, you need to behave in a way you feel is ethical. It's not always easy to see what is ethical. But if you apply the questions in this chapter, you will make the best decision when you face ethical problems.

Notes

1. William Lissy, "Employee Theft," *Supervision* (May 1, 1995), 17.

2. Rochelle Sharpe, "Labor Letter," *The Wall Street Journal* (June 15, 1994), A1.

3. Jill Cloud and Zeke Sarikas, "Software Piracy and the Small Business," *National Public Accountant* (September 1995).

4. Edmond Friley, "Ten Steps to a Near-Drug-Free Workplace," *Supervision* (June 1993), 6.

5. Thomas Garrett and Richard Klonoski, *Business Ethics,* 2nd Edition (Englewood Cliffs, NJ: Prentice-Hall, 1985).

6. Kenneth Blanchard and Norman Vincent Peale, *The Power of Ethical Management* (New York: Morrow, 1988), 47.

7. Archie Carroll, *Business and Society: Ethics and Stakeholder Management,* 3rd Edition, (Cincinnati: South-Western, 1993).

8. Larue Hosmer, *The Ethics of Management,* 3rd Edition, (Homewood, IL: Irwin, 1995).

9. Manuel Valasquez, *Business Ethics: Concepts and Cases*, 3rd Edition, (Englewood Cliffs, NJ: Prentice-Hall, 1991.)

10. Clarence C. Walton, *Corporate Encounters: Ethics, Law and the Business Environment* (Fort Worth, TX: Dryden Press, 1992), 101-102.

11. Rory J. Thompson, "Do the Right Thing-By Phone," *Information Week* (November 4, 1996), 10.

Chapter 13

Getting Ahead
on the Job

Two issues that usually concern new workers who've been on the job for a few months are pay increases and promotions. A more recent issue has been keeping a job when a company downsizes. There are no standard answers to these concerns, because each organization is different. Let's examine a few points about each of these issues.

You, Incorporated

A basic principle to thriving in the workplace today is to think of yourself as a business.[1] In Chapter 1, we looked at how you must be prepared to work as a core employee, temporary employee, or independent contractor. There are some basic principles you should follow to do this.

1. **Skills are your primary value to an employer.** Everything you do should emphasize your skills. Refer to the exercises in Chapter 7 to identify your skills.

2. **Skills are improved through experience and education.** Do jobs and tasks that give you this experience—even when you are frightened by the possibility of failure. Participate in educational activities that help you improve current skills.

3. **Market your skills.** Discuss skills you have with others. Use skills whenever possible to do tasks that help others notice you. Keep records of accomplishments that illustrate your skills.

4. **Stretch out and learn new skills.** The more skills you have, the more valuable you are. New skills can be learned through continuing education, company training programs, and higher education opportunities.

Getting a Raise

There are many general reasons organizations give pay raises.[2] Good pay helps businesses attract and keep good people. Raises are one way to reward good performance. The thought of more money can motivate employees to do a better job. But it's important to know when you can expect a raise. Unreasonable expectations can create misunderstandings between you and your employer. This, in turn, may cause you to lose interest in your job.

An organization's policy on pay increases usually is discussed at the job interview. If it hasn't already been explained to you, ask your supervisor to tell you how pay raises are determined. Below are some common instances when employers give pay increases.

■ **Completion of probation.** Probation can last from one to six months. Organizations often give raises after an employee has completed the probation period. Probation is considered a training period. After completing training, a worker has demonstrated the ability to do the work expected by the organization.

■ **Incentive increases.** Organizations using this method give raises according to the quality of work during a certain time period. Typically the work is evaluated every six months or once a year. Pay increases are based on evaluations and job performance. Organizations stressing teamwork might give pay increases based on the team's evaluation.

■ **Cost of living increases.** These are sometimes given to help employees offset inflation. Inflation is the increase in prices that lowers the value of the dollar. For example, if inflation rises 6 percent a year, at the end of that year $1 is worth only 94 cents. In this situation, an employer might give employees a 6 percent cost of living increase, so the buying power of their pay doesn't decrease.

■ **To keep employees.** Organizations may give highly valued workers pay increases to keep them from taking other jobs. If you receive a higher-paying job offer, it's appropriate to ask your employer for a raise. Don't use this approach unless you really have a better offer. In addition to damaging your credibility, your employer may not be able to afford a raise and tell you to take the other job.

■ **Reward for special efforts.** Sometimes employees take on added job responsibilities. Employers may reward this behavior by giving raises. Some organizations reward employees for learning new skills. The more skills you learn, the more money you earn.

■ **New assignments.** Raises normally are given along with new positions in the same organization, especially if it means a promotion to a more responsible position. Some businesses give increases based on the number of jobs a worker learns to do. The more jobs you are trained to do, the higher your pay.

When you start a new job, it's important to understand your employer's policy on pay increases. You are less likely to be disappointed by the size of your pay raises if you know what to expect. Knowing how your employer gives raises gives you an advantage and the motivation to work hard to receive a raise.

Key Definition

The Difference Between Wage and Salary

A *wage* is a specific amount of money earned for each hour worked. A *salary* is a flat payment per week or month, regardless of hours worked. Employers are required by federal law to pay hourly workers an overtime rate for hours worked in excess of 40 hours per week. Salaried workers usually are more highly paid because they don't receive overtime pay. It's possible for salaried employees to make less than hourly employees in the same organization if the hourly workers are working a lot of overtime.

Applying What You've Learned

Keith is a grill cook at Humpty Dumpty Hamburgers. He was told he would receive a raise after working for three months, and that he could be considered for another raise after six months. Keith has worked at the store for six months and still hasn't received a raise. Keith's supervisor has never talked with him about his job performance.

1. Do you think Keith deserves a raise? Why?

   _____

   _____

   _____

2. What approach should Keith take when asking for a raise?

   _____

   _____

   _____

Roberta has worked as a clerk for Golden Auto Parts for more than three years. Each year she receives a 5 percent raise. During the past year, inflation was 6 percent. Roberta does a good job, and her supervisor frequently praises her for her work. She is concerned that if she receives the same pay increase as in past years, it will not be enough for her to live on.

1. What percentage of pay increase should Roberta ask for?

   _____

   _____

   _____

2. How did you decide on the percentage?

_____

_____

_____

3. What approach should Roberta follow when discussing her raise?

_____

_____

_____

Barb has been a secretary at Newton Manufacturing Corporation for two years. Her performance appraisals have always been good and she has received a good pay raise each year she's been with the company. Recently, Barb saw an ad in the newspaper for a secretary. The advertised pay was $1,000 more per year than she is currently making. Barb believes she has the qualifications needed for the advertised job, and she is upset that she isn't being paid more by Newton. She plans to go into the office on Monday and tell her supervisor she could have a job that would pay her $1,000 more than she is making.

1. Do you think Barb's plan is a good one? Why?

_____

_____

_____

2. What plan would you suggest?

_____

_____

_____

Wayne is a bookkeeper for Hall's Home Oil Company. A few months ago his supervisor asked him to set up all the ledgers on a new computer system the company purchased. The new system has many advantages. The managers now receive financial reports that help save the company thousands of dollars each month. Wayne works hard to keep the computer system working. He has begun to wonder why he has been given this new responsibility, but no pay raise.

1. Do you think Wayne deserves a raise? Why?

    _____

    _____

    _____

2. What plan would you devise for Wayne to get a raise?

    _____

    _____

    _____

Getting Promoted

Not everyone wants a more responsible position, but many people do. Many organizations have limited the number of supervisory and management jobs available. This means that promotions are harder to get. However, promotions have several advantages, including these:

■ **Increased pay.** Normally, pay raises accompany promotions. However, sometimes a promotion to a salaried position is not much more money than an hourly worker earns with overtime pay.

■ **More respect.** Often, a promotion increases your status within the organization and in society.

■ **Better assignments.** You will do work that is more challenging. Lower-level positions usually require less ability, and sometimes workers become bored in these jobs.

■ **Improved self-esteem.** Your own self-esteem will improve when other people recognize you and your work. You'll feel better about yourself because of your success.

Promotions typically are based on two major criteria: seniority and merit.[3] Seniority refers to the amount of time on the job. Workers with more seniority often understand the organization and job better. Merit refers to the quality of job performance. Merit factors that are found most often in promoted employees include leadership, communication, and technical skills.[4] Both merit and seniority are considered when deciding which employee to promote. If specific skills or knowledge are required for the job, they are factored into the decision as well. If you want to be promoted, follow these tips:

■ **Keep track of job openings.** When a vacancy occurs, apply for the job. Talk to other workers. They usually know when someone is going to retire, be promoted, or leave for another job. Some companies post job openings by placing notices on a bulletin board, in the company newsletter, through memos, or by some other means.

■ **Talk to your supervisor.** Tell your supervisor you are interested in a promotion. Supervisors should know where the vacancies are in the company. If you have a good work history, your supervisor should be willing to give you a good recommendation.

■ **Notify the human resources department.** You should let the human resources or personnel department know you want a promotion. They will ask your supervisor about your job performance and keep you in mind when openings occur. In some organizations, you should notify your supervisor first. Find out the proper process for your organization.

■ **Create a network.** Networking refers to building friendships with coworkers in other departments. Secretaries are excellent people to include in your network because they have access to a great deal of information. Ask people in your network to notify you when they hear of possible job openings. For a network to work well, you must be willing to share information and help others in the network.

■ **Develop a good reputation.** Be a dependable, reliable employee and work hard. Get along with your coworkers. Become highly skilled in your job assignment. When you do these things, supervisors and managers will notice and remember you when a promotional opportunity arises.

■ **Create your own job.** It's possible to create a job for your own promotion. Look for ways to improve your organization. Make suggestions for accomplishing these improvements. Management might reward your creative thinking by placing you in a new job to carry out your suggestions.

When Promotions Occur

Promotions occur only when an organization has a job vacancy or the money to create a new job. You need to be patient about getting a promotion. However, when someone with less seniority than you receives a promotion, you should ask why. Discuss with your supervisor the difference between you and the other worker. Ask for suggestions to improve your performance. Take your supervisor's advice. It will help you compete for the next promotion.

1. List the skills a worker needs in order to get a promotion.

_____   _____

_____   _____

_____   _____

Applying What You've Learned

Lou has been a carpet layer at the Carpet Emporium for two years. He is dependable and gets along well with the other workers. He is very creative and often suggests time-saving methods of carpeting homes. Lou often criticizes and argues with the supervisor, but he always gets the job done.

Jan has worked at the Emporium for 16 months as a carpet layer. He also is dependable and gets along well with other workers. Jan took some classes in supervision at the local community college. He goes out of his way to help the supervisor and gets along well with him.

Business at the Carpet Emporium has been good. Management has decided to form an additional work crew to lay carpet. The department manager can't decide whether to promote Lou or Jan to supervise the new crew.

1. Who would you promote to the new supervisor's position?

_____

_____

_____

2. Explain the reasons for your selection.

_____

_____

_____

Jerry has been a secretary at Happy Acres Real Estate Agency for over two years and is currently taking a real estate course at the local junior college. He will complete the course in time to take the real estate license test next month. He learned through the office grapevine that one of the agents plans to retire within three months. Jerry talked to the manager about a promotion to an agent's position.

Bobbi came to work for the agency six months ago. She has her realtor's license but, because the agency wasn't hiring agents at that time, she took a position administering the deeds and titles in the office.

Jerry's information is correct. The agency is looking for another agent to replace the one who is retiring. The agency manager plans to promote from within the company, rather than hiring someone new. Jerry and Bobbi are the candidates.

1. Who would you promote to the agent's position?

_____

_____

_____

2. Why did you choose to promote this person?

_____

_____

_____

For the past two years, Marion has worked part-time for the Golden Years Home, a residential health care center. Marion first started working in the home as a volunteer when she was a junior high school student. During high school, she worked as a kitchen aide. Marion is studying to be a licensed practical nurse while working weekends at the health care center. The staff knows they can depend on Marion to be flexible. She has recently expressed an interest in working full-time.

Terry has been a volunteer at the home for two years and is a recent high school graduate. After graduation, she applied for a full-time position at the home and was hired as a nurse's aide. As a volunteer, Terry worked with the activities director during social times for the residents and helped plan many social events. Last summer, Terry traveled with the group to the Senior Citizens' Olympics, held in the state capital. The residents consider Terry an adopted grandchild.

Because of an increase in the number of residents, the health care administrator has decided to create a new staff position—assistant activities director. Both Marion and Terry are being considered for the position.

1. Who would you promote or hire for this position?

   _____

   _____

   _____

2. Why did you choose this person?

   _____

   _____

   _____

Charlene has been a waitress at the French restaurant, *Monsieur Jacques* for one year. Charlene is known for excellent service. Customers often ask to be seated at her tables, and she receives very good tips because of her speed in serving. However, she is impatient with the kitchen workers and those bussing tables when their work slows down her service. Charlene likes to work the business lunch crowd and usually refuses to work at other times. She knows many of the lunch customers by name and greets them as they are seated.

Alex has worked at *Monsieur Jacques* for two years. He is dependable and serves customers satisfactorily. Alex rarely visits with the customers, but he is always polite. He gets along well with coworkers and is willing to adjust to new work hours when needed. He even helps clear tables during rush hour. Last week the chef shared his secret crepe recipe with Alex. No one in the restaurant has known the chef to do this before.

Due to an increase in business, the restaurant manager has decided to add a *maitre de* during the lunch hour. This person would be responsible for greeting and seating customers, as well as honoring reservations. Charlene and Alex are both being considered for the promotion.

1. Who would you choose as the *maitre de?*

   _____

   _____

   _____

2. Why did you choose this person?

   _____

   _____

   _____

Career Development

The term *career development* refers to the process of reaching your personal goals in work and in life. Career development may not seem important during the first few years of your work experience, but you should understand the process early in your career and use it to achieve your highest possible level of success. There are several steps you can take to develop your career within an organization.

■ **Explore job possibilities.** Find out what kinds of jobs are available in your organization. Most organizations have jobs in a variety of occupations. Discover the types of jobs available by asking other workers about their jobs.

■ **Identify your skills and abilities.** Get to know yourself. Identify what you do best. Match your skills with jobs in the organization that require those skills.

■ **Know your values.** Know what you want from your career. People define success in various ways. You may define success by your career achievements, or your job may be secondary to family, friends, and recreation. How much time and energy do you want to give to your job? What do you need to accomplish in your career to support your values? These are important questions to answer before setting a career goal within the company.

■ **Set a goal.** Decide on your ultimate job goal within the organization. Make sure this goal is realistic. If you want to be president of the company, are you willing to devote the time and effort required to do it? It may take you several months or a few years before you know the organization well enough to set your career or job goal.

■ **Develop a career path.** What is the best way to advance to the position you want? There are several questions you should ask to find out:

1. What special qualifications are needed for the job? How much experience is required? Is a license or certification necessary for the job?

2. What kind of education is needed for the job? What major area of study corresponds with the job requirements? Is a college degree necessary?

3. How did other people get this job? What jobs did they have before they were promoted?

4. What type of classroom or on-the-job training is needed?

■ **Write your plan.** Use this information to create a career plan showing the progress you want to make in the organization. Put the plan in writing to motivate you to put forth more effort in reaching your goal. Include a timetable in your plan to show when you want to reach each job goal.

■ **Find a mentor.** A mentor is someone who takes a professional interest in you and advises you about your job. A mentor should be someone who is recognized and respected in the organization. Develop a mentor relationship by asking a person for help on a project or for advice about a situation. Another approach is to ask a person if he or she is willing to mentor you. Someone who enjoys helping you is more likely to be willing to do this.

■ **Keep a record of your accomplishments.** This is sometimes referred to as a portfolio. The human resources department or your supervisor probably keeps records of your work. However, don't expect them to keep a detailed record of your accomplishments. You should do this yourself. Any special skills you acquire, classes you attend, projects you complete, or ideas you suggest should be kept in a notebook or file. When you apply for promotions, use these records to help prove your qualifications.

■ **Review your plan.** Look over your plan every six months and review your progress. If you are pleased with your rate of progress, chances are you'll be motivated to continue to work hard to reach your goal. If you are unhappy about your progress, the review can help you plan what you need to do to make better progress.

■ **Change your plan when necessary.** Most plans aren't perfect. You will change and so will your goals. When this happens, develop a new plan. If the organization changes, you will have to change your plan. You may even have to leave your current job and go to another organization to meet your goals.

You must take responsibility for your own career development.[5] Companies won't do it for you, so you must take charge.

Leaving a Job

There are many reasons workers leave their jobs. The reasons for resignations can be summed up in three general categories.

1. **Job dissatisfaction.** Over time, you can become unhappy with a job because of personality conflicts or new management policies. Your career plans may not work out in the business. You will know you are not satisfied if you dread going to work every day.

2. **New opportunities.** Even when you're happy in your job, you might be offered another job that pays more or has more opportunities for promotion or better benefits. It can be difficult to decide what to do in these situations. However, you may very well decide to make a job change.

3. **Avoiding disaster.** You may want to leave a job because something bad will happen if you don't. The business may close, leaving you unemployed. The company may lay you off, and you can't afford to wait for a recall. Maybe you know the supervisor is unhappy with your work and is going to fire you. You may decide to leave the job before one of these events happen.

The average person changes careers almost seven times in his or her working life.[6] Chances are you will leave a job several times. You should understand how to change a career right from the start. Don't make a hasty decision that you'll regret later to leave a job. Here are some suggestions to help you prepare to leave a job.

■ **Have another job waiting.** Normally, you should not leave a job without having another one lined up. The best time to look for a new job is when you are employed. Leaving a job to look for a job puts you at a great disadvantage. Even when you find a job, it will be harder to bargain for better pay or position if you are desperate for a paycheck.

■ **Give reasonable notice.** The typical resignation notice is two weeks. Your employer may require a little more or less time than this. Find out from other workers the proper amount of time.

■ **Be tactful.** Don't resign in anger. You may be unhappy, but it isn't a good idea to tell your supervisor what you think is wrong with the organization. You need your employer for a reference and might even want to work for them again some day. Tell the supervisor the main reason you are leaving and that you aren't angry about the situation.

■ **What are the expectations?** Ask your supervisor what is expected during your remaining time on the job. There may be forms to fill out. Often the human resources department will conduct an exit interview to find out why you are leaving. Equipment, tools, uniforms, or other items must be returned. Be sure to get a written receipt showing you have returned the materials.

■ **Don't be disruptive.** Coworkers will wonder why you're leaving. Don't complain about your current employer to them. Let them know you've enjoyed working with them and hope to keep in touch. Leaving a job can be sad because you often leave friends behind. If you want to be remembered as a good worker and friend, act accordingly on your last days on the job.

The most important thing about leaving a job is to be fair to both your employer and yourself. Following the guidelines above helps create a good relationship with an employer. Your employer will be happy to give you a good reference and may even rehire you in the future if you treat them fairly.

Applying What You've Learned

Tamara has been a clerk in the post office for five years. She recently completed a four-year degree in accounting and was offered a position with a public accounting firm. The firm wants her to start work in two weeks. Tamara must decide how to resign from her job at the post office.

1. What steps should Tamara follow to resign from her current job?

_____

_____

_____

Eric is unhappy with his job. The supervisor has been giving him all the "dirty work." He has talked with his supervisor about the problem, but it hasn't helped. Eric found another job that pays better. The new employer wants him to start work immediately. Eric knows that his current employer expects at least two week's notice. However, Eric is so mad at his supervisor that he plans to call him on the phone to say he won't be in to work anymore.

1. Do you think Eric should do this?

_____

_____

_____

2. Explain the reasons for your answer.

_____

_____

_____

Summing Up

A job provides you with many opportunities, including pay raises, promotions, challenges, satisfaction, recognition, friendships, and a career. It's up to you to take advantage of these opportunities. By following the suggestions in this chapter, you can reach the career goals you set for yourself. Good luck on your journey!

You have an exciting future ahead. Your job is an important part of that future. It can provide you with the money you need to support a family, home, car, recreational activities, and lifestyle. To support your lifestyle, you must work hard at being successful in the job you have.

You have the ability to control your success by putting these skills into practice:

- Know what your employer expects from you, and do your best to meet those expectations.

- Be a dependable employee who is punctual and works whenever scheduled.

- Dress and groom yourself to fit into the workplace.

- Learn to do your job well. Take advantage of opportunities to improve your skills whenever training is offered. Be a lifelong learner.

- Believe in yourself and in your abilities. Know your skills and apply them. Work to improve your weaknesses.

- Recognize the important role your supervisor plays in your job success. Listen, complete assigned tasks, and volunteer to help your supervisor. Make yourself an important part of your supervisor's team.

- Cooperate and be friendly with coworkers. Your success can be built on the success of the work group.

- Participate in problem solving at work. Look for problems that you can help solve. Work with your supervisor and coworkers to solve problems.

- Be an honest employee. Your employer should be able to rely on your ethical behavior.

- Know what success on the job means for you. Plan your career and know how your current job fits into your plans. If you want pay raises and promotions, know what your employer expects you to do in order to get them.

Follow these practical, simple guidelines. Then say to yourself: "Look out world! Here I come!"

Notes

1. Derwin Fox, "Career Insurance for Today's World," *Training and Development* (March 1996), 61.

2. Douglas Hall and James Goodale, *Human Resource Mangement: Strategy, Design and Implementation* (Glenview, IL: Scott, Foresman, 1986).

3. Arthur Sherman, Jr., George Bohlander, and Herbert Chruden, *Managing Human Resources* (Cincinnati: South-Western, 1988).

4. Brian S. Moskal, "Promotions: Who Gets Them and Why," *Industry Week* (March 6, 1995), 45.

5. Richard Koonce, "Becoming Your Own Career Coach," *Training and Development* (January 1995), 18.

6. J. Michael Farr, *The Very Quick Job Search*, 2nd Edition (Indianapolis: JIST Works, 1996).